D1026469

ADAM TORRES

PRESENTS

VOLUME 6

BUSINESS LEADERS
EDITION

MISSION
MATTERS

World's Leading Entrepreneurs Reveal their
TOP TIPS TO SUCCESS

FEATURED AUTHORS:

Adam Nager	Jeff Norskog
Alan Pawlowski	Jeremy Hunt
Allan Hilsinger	Jessie Williams
Arnold Volker	Jim Downes
Charles Tyrrell	Joseph Catania
Demetra Bakas	Larry Phelan
Derek Gerber	Lenore Gregson
Don G. King	Preeti Tanwar
G Cole	Scott Shearin
Jason Shupp	Stephanie Limb

CENTURY
CITY

Century City, CA

Listen to our
PODCASTS

MISSION MATTERS

WE AMPLIFY STORIES

www.MissionMatters.com

© **2022 Adam Torres. All rights reserved.**

Copyright © 2022 by Mr. Century City, LLC. All rights reserved. No part of this book may be used or reproduced in any manner whatsoever without written permission except in the case of brief quotation embodied in critical articles and reviews.

For information, visit **www.MissionMatters.com**

Managing Editor:
James Ranson

Graphic Design:
Kendra Cagle

Century City, CA 90067
www.MissionMatters.com

The Mr. Century City Logo is a trademark of Mr. Century City, LLC.

ISBN 13: 978-1-949680-40-9

Mission Matters, Beverly Hills, CA

This publication is intended to provide general information regarding the subject matter covered. However, laws and practices often vary from state to state and are subject to change. Because each factual situation is different, specific advice should be customized to the particular circumstances. For this reason, the reader is advised to consult with his or her own adviser regarding that individual's specific scenario.

This book was created as a collaborative effort. Each author's opinion is solely their own. The authors have taken reasonable precautions in the preparation of this book and think the facts shown in the book are accurate as of the date it was written. However, neither the authors nor the publisher assumes any responsibility for any liability resulting from the use or application of the information contained in this book, and the information is not intended to serve as legal or professional advice related to individual situations.

DEDICATION

To the leaders who pay it forward.

TABLE OF CONTENTS

ACKNOWLEDGMENTS

Chirag Sagar, Co-Founder of Mission Matters

Matt Cook, Director of Agency, Mission Matters

Trent Lindsey, Podcast Producer, Mission Matters

The Sagar Family

James Ranson, Managing Editor

Christopher Kai, The Mathem Group

Jennifer Y. Chen, President & CEO of HBCS, Inc.

Dan Bienenfeld, President, KERV Interactive

Stella Song, CEO, Digital Luxury Agency

Eric Rosado, CEO, Karma Snack

Michael Douglas Carlin, Editor, Century City News

Dr. Ben Shamoiel, Chiropractor and Founder, The LA Chiropractor

Antonio De Shawn Spears, COO, City Global

Kendra Cagle, 5 Lakes Design

Keyan Razi, Founder & CEO, Impactnext

Patrick Reynoso, Chief Creative Officer, Digital Luxury Agency

Alice Yi, General Counsel, Digital Luxury Agency

INTRODUCTION

By **ADAM TORRES**

"Trust the process."

I've been given this advice many times in my life from mentors along the way. In my younger years it annoyed me a bit. What is this "process" and why should I "trust" it? Like many ambitious youths charging forward into the unknown, I thought that I deserved a level of success that was not realistic for my capabilities at that moment. For some of you reading this, you will smile, because you can relate. For others, you may be in the middle of the growth necessary to understand what it means to be "capable" of handling different levels of success and failure.

As I transition into different stages of my life, many of our readers have also been on this journey with myself and Mission Matters. To think it's already been 5 years since the first book was released, it makes me happy to think in another 5, 10, or even 20 years down the line I'll have the privilege of bringing fresh content, new perspectives and innovative stories to our loyal readers. To me, this is part of the "process" that I've been tasked with as I grow in my capabilities both as a leader and curator of content for our audience. This journey of bootstrapping a media company has not always been an easy one. Like all entrepreneurs, our company has faced the ups and downs and we've marched forward "trusting the process."

One of the things that has kept us strong as a company are the stories that we have the privilege to share. It surprises some that even though I've interviewed 4,000+ people, I still jump out of bed every morning anticipating who I get to interview next. The stories amaze me daily and I'm proud to bring this content to our audience. I can honestly say that the majority of my business education and ideas have come from the guests that have shared their stories on our shows. To think that this content is free to our audience makes me proud.

In our own small way I feel Mission Matters is adding to the brain trust of knowledge that we all benefit from by curating stories that have the power to inspire and move people to action. I'd like to share just a few of the interviews that caused me to reflect on what it means to "trust the process" in my own life with the hope that you may take away a piece of inspiration that causes you to march forward with whatever Mission that Matters to you.

Interviewing Aaron Alejandro, Executive Director of the Texas FFA Foundation (https://mytexasffa.org/) was a memorable experience for me. Aaron discussed the importance of agricultural education for youth and how the FFA (Future Farmers of America) provided a positive environment for personal growth for him when he was growing up.

Alejandro was ten when his father passed away, and when his mother found it challenging to control his escapades single-handedly, she enrolled him into an open-campus residential community. It proved to be a catalyst for Alejandro when he was placed in an agricultural science class and became a member of the FFA.

"While I struggled to make the life lesson connections through agriculture at first, I soon realized the program opened incredible doors of opportunity for personal and career success," he says. "Attending college was a challenge because of the lack of financial support. However, I believed in the fact that I lived in a country of opportunity and the iconic FFA jacket – which leveled the playing field – provided a path to academic success." His perseverance paid off, he notes, when he was elected state FFA president in 1985-86.

Serving as the Texas FFA's Development Executive for more than 20 years, he says he's "proud of the leadership development opportunities for students and teachers while helping facilitate $2.4 million in scholarships annually." *(Excerpt taken from story on* MissionMatters. com https://missionmatters.com/aaron-alejandro-discusses-the-importance-of-agricultural-education-for-todays-youth/)

Another interview that caused me to pause in my own life and reflect was when I had Bruce Parkman on the show. Bruce spoke about the Mac Parkman Foundation's (https://www.mpfact.com/) mission.

"The Mac Parkman Foundation was named after founder Bruce Parkman's late son, who died in September 2020. Bruce says he wants to spread awareness among parents about the secondary dangers of concussions in contact sports.

"I want to make parents aware of sub-concussive trauma, brain damage, and mental illness their children can come across due to contact sports," Parkman says. Through The Mac Parkman Foundation, he aims to spread awareness of the risks kids face when they play contact sports like football, volleyball, wrestling, soccer, and so forth while under the age of 14.

Parkman notes that while minor concussions may not have a major impact immediately, when they occur at such an early age, the young brain is still developing; he believes that such injuries can profoundly affect a child's mental or emotional growth well into later years. (*Excerpt taken from story on Mission* Matters.com https://missionmatters.com/mac-parkman-foundation-works-to-spread-awareness-of-the-dangers-of-adolescent-concussive-trauma/)

The final interview I'd like to share is when I had Reed Davis, Founder of the Functional Diagnostic Nutrition® Certification Course (https://www.functionaldiagnosticnutrition.com/) on the show.

Davis tells the story of founding Functional Diagnostic Nutrition Certification, a health coach training program with 3,000+ students in over 50 countries, after learning to identify healing opportunities within a subset of patients who were not seeing results from traditional medical treatments they had been following.

"Many of our patients came to us after seeing two, four or even eight practitioners prior to coming into our wellness center. They were stuck in the cycle of trial and error with treatments that weren't working for them. Being non-medically licensed nutritional practitioners, we had the opportunity to treat the whole person by finding out what was really wrong, instead of just chasing symptoms or managing the disease," said Davis.

Through running thousands of laboratory tests on thousands of clients, the framework for Functional Diagnostic Nutrition®

Certification was born. The methodology draws from a comprehensive investigation including the H.I.D.D.E.N. formula, which stands for hormone, immune, digestion, detoxification, energy production, and nervous system balance, and is used to assess this constellation of underlying conditions found upstream." (*Excerpt taken from full story on* MissionMatters.com https://missionmatters.com/reed-davis-finds-healing-opportunities-through-functional-diagnostic-nutrition/)

The interviews I shared above are examples of Missions that are led by determined individuals focused on creating positive change. Aaron is focused on our youth and agriculture, Bruce is focused on helping to educate a sports ecosystem that is many times unknowingly putting our youth at risk, and Reed is looking after our physical health through training practitioners in his certification course. Though each mission is different, at their core is focus to help others even when at times experiencing personal hardship. To take a situation and to use it for good.

As you read this book you will encounter stories of perseverance and vision. I encourage you to reflect on how your own vision and perseverance can help you get out of your comfort zone. Don't resist change, tackle a problem from a different perspective, just say yes, reinvent yourself. Comfort is something that can sneak up on you. Whether in your professional life as an entrepreneur or executive, or in your personal life as a member of a household, it's one of those things that is easy to succumb to.

Over the last two years, many of us have been jarred from our comfort zones in one way or another due to the pandemic. Some have experienced tremendous growth in their businesses, while others were devastated by events that were not necessarily under their control.

At Mission Matters, we are always exploring new show formats and vehicles to help individuals amplify their stories and broadcast them to the world. One of the major takeaways from the worldwide paradigm shift we've experienced is to not get complacent. To not let comfort creep into our lives. To continue to strive for innovation. For new ideas. New perspectives. Alternative ways of thinking that add value to the marketplace.

This book, our latest edition of Mission Matters Business Leaders Vol. 6, is filled with innovators that continue to push forward in good times and bad. It's my hope that the lessons that fill these pages will inspire you to do the same.

To your success,

Adam Torrey

P.S. If you'd like to share your story, visit **MissionMatters.com** to apply to be a guest on our show!

CHAPTER 1

PERSISTENCE DEFEATS RESISTANCE

By **ADAM NAGER**

I learned from a very early age that persistence defeats resistance. I had to.

I dropped out of high school without obtaining my GED. I have no college degree. I could have let myself be limited by the belief that without an education, I wasn't going to go anywhere, that I wouldn't be successful. Instead, when somebody said no to me, I chose to find a way to get somebody else to say yes.

Early in my career, before I was an entrepreneur, I had to figure out a way to get a job without a school diploma or college education. So I wrote a really solid resume and sent it over to a hiring manager. But I didn't just leave it at that. If the hiring manager wasn't there, I called, texted, emailed, and knocked on the door of the hiring manager's office at least half a dozen times to get their attention. I needed the hiring manager to know who I was, to give me a chance to sell myself outside of a piece of paper. I needed to break down the resistance so they said, "you know what, this guy Adam is extremely persistent, let's give him a call."

Throughout my years in business, I figured out that if I am persistent enough, I can break down the resistance of potential clients, giving them the confidence and comfort to allow me into their organizations to support them, coach them, and work with them, to ultimately build our collective success.

Without persistence, I simply would not be where I am today, the founder and owner of 7 companies with 150+ employees across three continents. Today, I'm proud to support clients in over 40 states, helping thousands of doctors nationwide every month.

That doesn't mean that I haven't faced my fair share of resistance and challenges.

Which begs the question, what does it actually mean to be persistent? What does it look like and how do you navigate it? How do you know when enough is enough and when to walk away?

I hope the experiences I've had can help you to navigate resistance and truly understand what persistence entails.

What Does Persistence Look Like?

One of the hardest things in business is landing your first client.

My largest business today is a medical billing company which I started in 2008. At the time, I was working for a Department of Defense contracting firm. With no college education, my GED recently acquired at 21 years old, I was selling to doctors' offices-people who had literally spent over a decade getting university degrees. You can imagine that I was not exactly taken seriously on paper.

There was a particular office that I had called at least a dozen times. I knocked on the door, dropped off materials, and called the practice over, and over, and over again. Around the twelfth time, the doctor finally returned my call and said, "alright, enough is enough, come on in and let me hear how you may be able to support me."

I had finally broken the resistance. That thirty-minute conversation was all I needed to sell myself, to show my capabilities to this doctor, and to really shine.

This was one year into my business. A whole year in business and my relentless persistence had paid off. I had finally landed my first client.

I can say that without a doubt if it wasn't for that doctor calling me back, I would not be in business today. You remember that it was 2009 — the recession had just hit, and I'd already been in business for a year without booking a single client. At that point, I thought I was done. My business was over. But despite the fact that I was just about ready to throw in the towel, I stayed consistent and persistent in knocking on the door, trying to break through…and it paid off.

Breaking down the resistance of one was all it took. Within three weeks, I landed clients two and three, and better yet, these clients were all referrals. That's what has built my business into what it is today.

I'm often asked how many emails, phone calls, office visits, or text messages it takes to break down the resistance. The truth is, there is no magic number. It takes as many times as it takes.

Which begs the question, how do you know when it's time to remain persistent and when it's time to let it go?

How Do You Know Whether It's the Right Thing to be Persistent About?

I'm in healthcare today for a few reasons. I'm a Type 1 diabetic and I have a history of lower back issues, so health is naturally very important to me. But it's not just that.

When I was 21 years old and working in retail management, I injured my back so severely I sought out a chiropractor, miraculously finding one willing to see me right away on a Sunday. Over the course of my treatment, my chiropractor managed to completely heal me. The reward for his efforts? A check from the insurance company for less than the cost of the postage stamp on the outside of the envelope.

That was his total and final payment as paid by my insurance company to his practice. It made me furious! This amazing medical professional had given me everything he had, literally fixed my body and my life, and the insurance company thought his work was worth less than the cost of a postage stamp. This anger at how my chiropractor was treated, built a level of passion inside me for helping healthcare providers get what they deserve for their hard work.

You see, there is an undeniable connection between passion and persistence. If you aren't passionate about something, you can only be persistent for so long. But with passion, you can consistently show persistence without feeling the strain of it.

The right time to walk away from persistence is when you have lost your passion.

Your passion may waver from time to time and that's okay. If you do lose the passion, you have to either reignite it or move on to something different.

"Everyone has a plan until they get punched in the mouth." - Mike Tyson

The question is when you get punched in the face, do you still have the passion because you remember your why? Or have you lost your why because the passion's been knocked out of you?

When you know the why behind your passion, maintaining persistence, even when the passion gets knocked out of you every so often, won't be so difficult.

Navigating Different Types of Resistance

There are many different types of resistance that you'll face in business. You'll face resistance from clients based on timing, financial commitment, or fear of change. You'll inevitably face resistance from other people and even your own thoughts. The important thing is to let these resistances fuel your persistence, instead of extinguishing it completely.

After my success with the aforementioned doctor's office, my business started getting a lot of inbound inquiries or leads. Oftentimes, you'll call these leads back and they won't answer, forcing you to leave a message. Many people would leave it at that and wait for the lead to never get back to them. But this is a complete waste of opportunity. In business, it's all about the follow-up.

One of the biggest contracts I signed in my early days of business was from a lead that I had called half a dozen times, a woman named Mrs. Brandt. On the seventh call, she finally picked up and said, "I've seen you have called several times. I appreciate your persistence. You've caught me at the right time."

I signed a contract with Mrs. Brandt that consequently generated $30,000 of monthly revenue for my business.

Mrs. Brandt's resistance was not that she wasn't interested in my product or service. Her resistance was that on the previous six times I'd tried to contact her, she wasn't available to take the call, she was busy or focused on other things.

One of the key things to remember when applying persistence is that we are all human. Life is busy and our to-do lists are never-ending. Show your human side, empathize with your leads and ask questions like, "when is a good time to reach out?" and most importantly, stay persistent until you either get a yes or a no.

Fear of the unknown is another notable contributor to resistance. Your clients may be fearful to move forward when they don't know or understand aspects of whatever you're offering them — like what it's going to cost them, what they have to lose, or what the opportunity actually looks like.

In these situations, persistence is identifying the risks, outlining pros and cons, and showing them how this change can help them to better align with their goals. You can even outline the absolute worst-case scenario to help them realize that if things go belly-up, it's actually not that bad. When you obtain clarity and knowledge around the unknown, it's not so unknown anymore and the fear will dissipate.

Another common form of resistance you'll face in business, and in life generally, is the resistance of other people or voices in your own life.

When I started out in the healthcare industry, I had no shortage of people ready to tell me what I didn't know about the industry and how I could easily fail, or how I didn't have the pipeline or the funds to get such a business off the ground. And to that I said, "watch me."

I believe that listening to and hearing what other people have to say is important. But following what other people say is not, especially when they are not somebody of influence in your life. It doesn't make sense to take advice from people who haven't done the thing that you want to do. Be willing to take what other people think, as what they think. It's nothing to do with you or who you are. What you're doing doesn't have to make sense to them, as long as it makes sense to you.

Use these situations as fuel to build your own undeniable resistance to the outside. Adding your passion into the mix will only add fuel to the fire of your perseverance.

In the instance that the resistance is coming from within your own thoughts, get yourself some support. Finding a coach, mentor, or group of like-minded people to support you, is paramount to overcoming your own resistance.

Leaning on somebody who has already been through the minefield is a great way to break down your resistance. They have stepped on the mines already. They have experienced setbacks and frustrations along the way and can help you avoid the same fate. If you are willing and able to trust them, they can guide you through to the other side of the landmine unscathed.

Persistence vs. Production

There is often a lot of conflation between the idea of being persistent and the notion of being a workaholic. Many people believe that you have to hustle 24/7 to be persistent or successful but for me, this is not true.

Persistence is not based on production–they are two different things. Production is what you do on a daily basis. Persistence is your willingness to do what others aren't willing to do.

Production is putting a schedule together and following it persistently. It's being deliberate about what you do in your life, identifying goals to reach toward, planning ahead, and staying consistent. If you are not persistently doing something in your business every single day, you are automatically going backward.

When you are both productive and persistent within your business, you'll start to build momentum. Momentum is one of the hardest things to gain and one of the easiest things to lose in business. This is another reason why it's so important to know your why. When your passion is strong enough, the production in your business comes easy, inevitably leading to persistence and the steady growth of momentum.

Summary

If you want to make a change, to be different than others, to succeed to a higher level, you need to be willing to do what those other people aren't willing to do or have already stopped doing. Take it from a guy that started out without a GED or college education, it is nothing to do with capabilities. It is all about being productive in your business every day. Continuously call that practice, call that doctor, be persistent.

Generally speaking, the message or service I'm delivering isn't very different from any of our competitors. I'm just the guy who has offered it more persistently than anyone else. That's why I win. And it's how you can win, too.

CHAPTER 2

FOUR OPERATIONAL TOOLS FOR DRIVING BUSINESS VALUE

By **ALAN PAWLOWSKI**

I often speak on the topic of business valuations to various business owners and entrepreneurial audiences. One of the first questions I ask every room is "who in the audience knows the value of their business?" Consistently, approximately 20% of the room raises their hand.

The next question I ask is "why are you attending my presentation?" Most of the answers I get from audience members tend to do with wanting to sell or transition out of their businesses. Maybe they're getting near exit age, thinking about succession planning, dealing with illness, having a dispute with a partner, or just wanting to do something different — all valid and logical reasons to transition out of a business.

Do you see the disconnect? If 80%-100% of the audience wants to sell their business, but only 20% of that audience actually knows the value of their business, then at least 80% of that room is going to potentially lose money.

Why don't most business owners know the value of their own businesses?

Well, many times the owner has an idea of what they THINK the business is worth. But unfortunately, most tend to see valuation as simply assets and inventory on the balance sheet, and it's much more complex than that. Earnings, customer risk concentrations, strategic buyers vs. financial buyers, intellectual property, real property, and a dozen other factors play into it.

What this means is that unless a valuation expert or vetted valuation methodology has been used to derive that number for the business owner, the owner's perception of their business's value is *universally overstated.*

In fact, working with this kind of professional or system is so important that I'm not even going to discuss or explain how to determine the value of your business here. That is well beyond the scope of this chapter and would take much more space than we have here.

So let's all assume that you have worked with a valuation expert to determine the value range of your business and understand the basic principles behind your business valuation. Because once you have a clear sense of your business's actual value, you can start using the following four tools to **increase that value.**

Business Value Tool #1: The Finish Line

How much is enough? Not just for the sale of the business value, for the whole enchilada! What do you want your personal net worth to be later in life when you decide to lift your foot off the accelerator a bit, or even hit the brakes? This is the "enough" to get you well across the finish line, maintaining the lifestyle you are accustomed to (or want to get accustomed to), and maybe leave a bit behind for the next generation.

I always ask my clients if they have thought about that figure in the context of their personal balance sheet or investment portfolio(s) in any early-stage exit strategy discussions. How much do you need from your business sale in addition to all other financial instruments to feel comfortable to get through the golden years or fund the next chapter in life? Big question, to be sure, and usually takes quite a bit of time and self-examination for one to determine. But once we know what that number is, we can then solve the following formula:

FLH = BV + O

FLH - *Finish Line Happiness*
BV - *Business Value*
O - *Other Net Personal Investments*

Or for those of us who like algebra:

BV = FLH - O.

That is, the business value you need to reach is equal to your Finish Line Happiness total desired net worth number minus any other personal investments that will contribute to that number. There you have it. Your own Personal Business Valuation Formula (**PBVF**)!

I was talking to a new client some years ago and we were talking about what he thought the business was worth. Quite confidently, the client stated that the business was worth $8,000,000 and that would be the minimum sale price required to sell the business. So he had a self-determined BV number of $8,000,000 to accomplish his desired FLH total net worth

After we did a market valuation, we determined the business value range was in the low to mid $3,000,000's. That was a very large gap. The client also wanted a near-term exit from the business and to sell the business as soon as possible. So there would not be a lot of time to grow the business value, especially by $5,000,000.

When I broke the bad news to the client, I asked if there was any way to lower the BV number and base it on what he and his family needed for end-of-life happiness, not what was a desired business sale price. We ended up meeting with the family and their investment advisors to determine what the business valuation "needed" to be to solve the above formula.

The business's "needed value" ended up being about $4,250,000. Now this gave us something to work with. We implemented a business improvement strategy in conjunction with an aggressive retirement savings plan and just under three or so years later we took the business to market, sold it to a strategic buyer, and solved the Finish Line Happiness formula for the client. Success!

Tool #1, The Finish Line, is a powerful tool and you can not start using it too early in your entrepreneurial career. Work with your team of professionals and determine what your FLH "enough" desired total net worth goal is. Once you get to "enough," you certainly don't have to sell your business. But once you do reach that goal, you will have the peace of mind that your later-in-life financial goals are met. And as you grow your business's value, Tool #1 will be an invaluable way to measure and ensure you always know where you are with regard to what may be one of your most important goals in life, your desired net worth.

Business Value Tool #2: The Drivers

The process of getting a valuation is educational. You learn the financial aspects that drive your business's value (earnings, sales, margin, EBITDA, inventory, etc.) along with the non-financial business value drivers (customer profiles, intellectual property, brand, employees, etc.).

By knowing your business value and understanding its value drivers, you now have a tool to assist with business decision-making. Decisions made in and for your business can then improve, or at least be value-neutral, to the business valuation. That correlation and awareness is both powerful and strategic.

I helped a business owner sell a series of retail pharmacies a few years ago. The buyers were national franchises, names we would all recognize. Interestingly, the valuation methodology represented by all buyers who placed offers was simply a multiple of pharmacies' annual prescription revenue. The value had nothing to do with the retail sales, durable rental equipment sales or rentals, or oxygen sales business. This wasn't a mistake or oversight, incidentally — it was actually how business valuation worked in that industry. But the business owner didn't understand those valuation drivers and metrics throughout the years of growing and operating her business.

The business owner had a very large inventory of durable medical equipment along with general retail stock, all of which consumed resources to maintain, but none of which improved the value or marketability of the business. Had the business owner known the industry valuation method, she could have sold down some of that inventory prior to taking it to market or may have just elected to focus more energies on prescription sales versus other retail and equipment sales and rentals over the years prior to exit planning.

Not all business decisions will be value-neutral or positive. Being aware of your specific business value drivers just adds another valuable reference point tool to the business owner's decision-making matrix.

Tool #2, The Drivers, shows why it's so important to know your business value methodology and value drivers. When you do, you can assess all decisions as to whether they are additive, neutral, or deductive from the business value. This tool allows you to be more strategic in decision-making at every level, especially when preparing for a sale.

Business Value Tool #3: The Speed

We look at varied and diverse characteristics when reviewing our traditional investment portfolios, but ultimately, we all look most closely at return on investment (ROI) as a measurement of performance for our investments and personal wealth In the context of this writing, ROI is the measurement of how fast we will get to our coveted FLH economic status illustrated in Tool #1, The Finish Line, above.

Professional investors like private equity groups are all about measuring, and committing to, a return on investment for their investors, all based on various strategies creating a positive change in the acquired business values many times based upon a subsequent consolidation and sale.

So why don't we as entrepreneurs measure and closely track the ROI for our own businesses (likely our largest single investment as noted above) like professional investors do?

I believe there are many reasons for the glaring disparity in our business performance measurement and traditional investment performance culture. Emotional connection to the business allows for relaxed scrutiny. Viewing the business as not really a business but more of a hobby, makes ROI less, if at all, relevant. The single most common reason why business owners do not closely track change in enterprise value is the predominant lack of ability to measure and credibly compare the change in the value of the business (their investment) over a period of time.

In other words, it can be as difficult to accurately gauge how your business's value is changing over time without a starting value in the first place. It is easy to measure the change in value of a publicly-traded stock because of the perpetual availability of the present value of that same stock, or your starting point.

As assumed above, you know your business valuation. If you do not, determine it as of the end of your last fiscal year with a valuation professional. With this starting point well in hand, you will now be able to credibly measure the change in the business value as compared to previous period(s). But that's not the tool. The tool is keeping track of your valuations every year and computing the percentage change or ROI year over year.

This can be a compelling exercise. You are now benchmarking your business, its teams, market, process, brand, etc. and ultimately your decision making performance against previous business periods, but more importantly, against traditional and alternative investments options and opportunities using your most finite resources, your time and your capital

Tool #3, The Speed, tells how quickly our business (investment) value is changing by measuring the change in business value as compared to a previous period, and subsequently, your ROI

Does it really make sense for me to have a large amount of my personal wealth and time tied up in a business? Impossible question to answer...unless you have Tool #3, The Speed, to help you look at the big picture and contrast the performance of your business with other possible options.

Business Value Tool #4: The Call

Have you gotten that call? Or have you gotten that letter? This is one of the most recurring questions I field from my clients. The call or letter may have sounded or read something like this:

"Ms. Smith, I have been retained by a vetted and qualified buyer who is looking for acquisitions in your industry. You are a business on a shortlist of targets we have been hired to contact and to further gauge any interest for possible sale of some or all of your business's assets, stock, etc."

Oh, by the way, those calls and letters are many times real, not a hoax. They often come from legit M&A professionals working for buyers who are ready and able to acquire your business. They are usually a good, well-capitalized, strategic buyer. Good news, right?

Yes, but there's also bad news. Those buyers are sophisticated buyers running a strategic acquisition process and are likely going to pay a fair "strategic value" within an industry-established range. Not an off the M&A chart record-setting sale price for a business (what we all dream about when we lay in bed that first night after a call or letter is received, right?).

In other words, buyers may not be looking to pay you your BV from Rule #1 above to solve your FLH equation. They're going to try to pay you as little as they can (obviously). In the end, the process will likely produce a fair price transaction, though probably not a great one.

Two things that strategic buyers hope for when approaching a business to acquire is that you probably don't actually know what your business is worth, and that you'll be so distracted by their offer that you won't consider the fact that you might be able to get a better price from a different buyer, or how to even go about doing so.

As a buyer, they want to isolate their target (you) and control the narrative around a possible sale. But as an owner and potential seller, you want to be talking to as many would-be-buyers as possible and create a competitive environment, ultimately driving up the price.

Don't you hate when you are on a car lot and someone walks up to the car you want just before you are ready to tender an offer and start negotiations? Why do we hate it? Because the opening offer likely just went up due to the presence of additional interest or competition. If that person actually makes an offer as well, well, you all know what happens next. The dealer is eating steak that week, not hamburgers because the final sale price went up, a lot. We want to be the car dealer. We want multiple bidders. We want those emotional responses from buyers when selling our business.

So what do you do when you get the call or letter inquiring to buy your business? Tool #4, The Call, gives you the ability to strategically respond to those acquisition calls and letters.

You are now empowered with the knowledge of the value of your business, and more importantly, you know from Tool #1, The Finish Line, whether the sale of the business today will be "enough" to meet your big picture or later-in-life financial goals or needs. You can now choose to ignore the call or letter entirely, or possibly even respond.

If you do decide to entertain a dialogue regarding the sale of your business, one possible way to respond could be:

"We are not currently for sale, nor do we have plans to sell in the near term. We track our business's strategic value, though, so if you are interested in discussing offers above high strategic market value, we would then be glad to initiate discussions."

Clearly, your response, or lack thereof, should represent what a success or desirable outcome may look like to you. I advise all my clients to respond in this way unless they are in fact willing and ready to go to market and sell the business right away.

The reality of starting that dialogue is a large commitment. I tell my clients that once that process starts three things likely happen and none of them are good: 1- You are now moderately to significantly distracted from your business for an extended period of time. 2- The process will likely be expensive. 3- During the process, you might get your heart set on selling, and it may not happen. Getting my clients to have that same entrepreneurial flame after a failed process is many times challenging, if even possible.

Using Tool #4, The Call, is the most powerful tool presented here today. Knowing when you and the business are ready to go to market to sell, and by YOU controlling the process and narrative throughout, ensures the highest likelihood of your desired outcome. Businesses are sold every day that respond to "The Call", but not for what they could have sold for if not handled properly.

Closing

My tools are proven to help positively drive your business enterprise value.

- **Tool #1 - The Finish Line:** Know how much you need the value to be before selling your business.
- **Tool #2 - The Drivers:** Know what influences the value of your business and use that knowledge as part of your decision-making strategy.
- **Tool #3 - The Speed:** Know the performance of your business and assess its ROI regularly to help assess future resource allocation decisions.
- **Tool #4 - The Call:** Know how to handle purchase solicitations and offers and how to avoid not selling too early, undervaluing your business, or having the end of a long successful ride end up being a bad experience.

This is the first time I have organized my business-value-related tools together. They all work. All have been tried, tested, and used for years by various clients, all with positive feedback and results. This book is the first time I have started connecting even more M&A dots and interrelating and connecting my practitioner tools. For those of you reading this that have used my tools in the past, thank you for the beta testing.

With these additional tools, you are now better prepared to fight the daily battle we call business and to also operate your business at a higher and more sophisticated level. I am certain using the four tools will help you strategically grow your business value well past your wildest dreams and Finish Line Happiness value, of course!

CHAPTER 3

GIVE IT A TRY

By **ALLAN HILSINGER**

We live in a world full of opportunities. They're limitless and around every corner. In this chapter, I'll take you through my key tenets of seizing an opportunity: Find a need, create the solution, embrace the challenge, do your homework, and execute.

Whether you're starting a business or taking a risk in your personal life, there will be voices from all directions telling you how to do things, and why what you're attempting isn't going to work. Ignore the negativity. You have to listen to your own inner itch instead. One of my best friends told me my idea for Guard Well wouldn't work. Well, guess who we now pay a very substantial amount of sales commission to each year? That same guy!

Find a need

The only way you're going to be able to successfully elevate a company, or yourself, is by finding something that provides value to other people. Let me take you back to my first ever business to show you what I mean.

I was 9 or 10 years old. Growing up I swam for the local swim club swim team in the summer. Next door to the pool there was a

country club with an 18-hole golf course and a lake. After swim practice, I threw on my old converse high tops, grabbed some garbage
bags, and slid into the lake. And it was nasty...probably six inches of
pure muck lined the bottom of the lake. But it was LOADED with golf
balls, by the handfuls. Pure gold. I took two garbage bags of golf
balls out of the pond the first day...and managed to piss off several
dozen golfers as well, but hey, risk and sacrifice is part of the gig,
right? Success is not always glamorous, in fact it rarely is to me. But
I clearly remember how I felt that first day I was in that lake 40 years
ago. I felt like the King of the World.

I cleaned up the golf balls and headed to a smaller, nine-hole golf
course nearby to open up shop. I already knew the course clubhouse
was selling their balls for 75 cents apiece and three for two bucks.
I had them beat: 50 cents apiece or three for a buck. I'd sit by the
fence on the 7th tee box and sell these balls until I was all out. Then
go back to my supply chain, only now it would be in the evening. I'd
hop (slide) into the lake in the evening rather than the day. Fewer
golfers, less chance of getting in trouble, a better system. In business you ALWAYS need to look for tweaks, improvements...a little bit
better way. It doesn't have to be world-changing - unlike the first day
in the lake - but small improvements over time create success and my
machine was starting to become well oiled.

That is...until the manager at the nine-hole course took a stand.
He advised our swim club manager that I was stealing all of the golf
ball sales from the course clubhouse and I was trespassing. I was cutting into their profits at 10 years old. If I was caught on the course
again I'd be in trouble. I took a big hit, shrugged it off, and changed
course, finding new opportunities.

And that's where it started. I've never looked back, ever. Not once. There are just too many things to do. One thing that always amazes me is that the basic business principles of my "first business" are very much the same as any organization I've started or led. Like I always ask the kids I coach in youth sports after each game - win, lose or draw - "What did we learn?" Always learn.

Create a solution

Sometimes, a great idea means helping someone find a better way to do the things they already do, even without any sort of new technique or invention.

99% of the organizations we work with at Guard Well have the same problem: a ton of old IT hardware lying around and no good way to dispose of it. Old laptops and hard drives store sensitive data that a company doesn't want to just end up in a landfill or in a dumpster out back. In the past, companies have brought in a recycling service to drill the hard drives so the data is not accessible, and then the metal is scrapped. The organization might pay $8 or $10 per computer to get them drilled or wiped and only make back $1 selling the scraps. It's an expense and a liability.

When I first heard about this process, I thought, why don't we partner with the organization, buy the hardware from them, wipe their drives for free, and then sell them? We'd be accomplishing the same thing as the recycling companies – getting rid of the gear and eradicating the sensitive data – but instead of the organization getting $1 per laptop, we'll give them $10 for it because we're going to sell it instead of just drilling the drive. Plus we will save them the expense by wiping the drives for free. It benefits them, it's more revenue for us when we sell the hardware, and it's also better for the environment because we're not putting perfectly good equipment into a scrap metal heap.

We didn't invent the recycling world, and we didn't invent the repurposing world. All we did was take people who were not getting what they should've been getting for their assets, and give them a better option. Our list of clientele for this service grows weekly. It's another example of my belief that you don't have to be the smartest person in the room, or have the most perfect idea. You just have to do something better than it's already being done.

Embrace the challenge

Nothing about my journey has been easy. For the first four years after founding Guard Well, I lost money. At times it was brutal. I saw my way through the tough times with a simple motto: Be patient. Don't panic. Stay positive. We have a great plan. If you have a great plan, as I did, then you just have to keep your foot on the gas pedal. If you get to the point where you know it's not going to work, then you have to go do something else or retool, but you need to be absolutely sure that you've seen your plan through before you evaluate the results. However, don't confuse a great plan with a perfect plan that never needs to be improved upon. You will always need to learn, adjust and improve along the journey.

But if I'm really going to talk about embracing the challenge, I need to talk about snow. I've spent over 30 of my 50 years on this earth going to work when it snowed. I had my neighborhood route as a kid. I never missed a snowstorm, ever. My clients relied on me and I was going to show up no matter what. Eventually I was old enough to use a snowblower, then my dad's tractor, and then his Jeep. After my accounts were taken care of I'd sled and play with my neighbor buddies. Work first, then play.

In college, my friends would work at the bookstore for $4/hour. I would get chastised for not having a "job." But when the snow would fall I'd head out and make over $1000 per night. I'd make $100 per hour compared to $4 per hour. Eventually that $100 per hour turned into $1000 per hour, cool trucks, big parking lots, and LOTS of salt. There is big money in spreading salt in the hilly, icy midwest cities that need to function as normally as possible during snowstorms. At one point I was spreading over 30,000 pounds of salt per storm. I've never added it up but over those decades I made way over $1,000,000 playing in the snow, easily.

Sounds easy, right? Wrong. Sure, a quarter of a century into my snow plowing life I was making at times over $100,000 a season as a side job. But it didn't happen overnight and it didn't happen by accident...it happened over decades of commitment. I never missed a storm, not in all of those years. It means not traveling all winter and if you do keep a close eye on the weather in case you need to head home early - which I've done several times - or cancel your trip entirely - which I've also done several times. But I had to be there for my clients, no excuses.

One time I was out 32 hours straight, came home to sleep four hours, headed back out for 16 hours, slept for 8, and went back out for 8. All while driving a half-ton Chevy stick shift. It had to be done so I did it. I had a family, employees, and clients that were counting on me to pull through. I needed that money to pay the bills and eventually pay my house payment while I was starting Guard Well. Snow, that was my pathway to success.

Failure is going to happen inevitably, but the feeling of success is so unmatched that it's worth every swing and a miss. There are defining moments in life, not just in business, where the exhilaration of something finally working makes you forget about the years of hard work it took to get to your destination. I'm lucky enough to have had several of them, including when Guard Well first turned a profit. None of those moments would have been possible if I hadn't embraced the challenges along the way.

Do your homework

Hopefully it's come across by this point that I haven't had the most traditional entrepreneurial path. From my childhood golf ball business to my main professional focus the Identity Protection and Management firm, and the shoveling, salting, mowing, landscaping, vending, and real estate gigs in between, I've been involved in many industries. Heck, I was even involved in two Ponzi schemes without knowing it! Different industries come with the downside of sometimes starting over in an industry that I know next to nothing about. But those same basic business principles almost always apply.

After college, I started a lawn mowing business and I had an absolute blast. I'd put thousands of flyers up on mailboxes around town, canvassing entire neighborhoods with my friends that worked for me. The mowing business took off and was an immediate success, but once the summer started we had a severe drought. And no rain means no mowing, which means no business!. I decided that I'd better learn how to landscape as well, because droughts could happen every year. Remember that talk about always improving? I had to go from being a kid with a marketing degree out cutting grass to someone who knew the intricacies of professional landscape design. And quickly. It turns out college wasn't the last time I'd have to do my homework.

On Sundays, I went to the local nursery for hours at a time to study the plants. I walked around memorizing their names, their functions in a landscape, and what size they would grow to. I wasn't an expert by any means, but soon I figured out that if I could act like I was an expert, people might be convinced that I knew what I was talking about. It turns out that strategy works – the landscaping enterprise turned into an annual six-figure business over the next six years. All from the power of doing my homework.

Don't do it alone

Just because I've been my own boss all my life doesn't mean I've done things alone. It's quite the opposite, actually. At every step of the way in all my businesses, I've surrounded myself with great associates, clients, and friends. When I was 19 and running my first real business of pavement seal coating it wouldn't have been possible if I hadn't been able to buy an old truck off my dad, or if my friend's dad hadn't owned the small pharmacy whose lot was the first I seal coated. I knew nothing about landscape design but I found people to help me who did. I knew nothing about building a Dollar General building but I hired people who did. I knew nothing about identity protection but I interviewed the biggest players in the industry and partnered with people who did.

You find out over the years the things you are good at and more importantly the things you are not good at. Because you are not good at everything, I'm living proof of that. You have to be willing to ask for help and when the time comes, return the favor. You've heard the saying, "To whom much is given…much is expected." This help thing is most certainly a two-way street.

I'm like many people who have found success, it would not have been possible without the dozens or hundreds of helping hands along the way. Those folks deserve much of the credit. From the homeowner that gave a 10-year-old his snow shoveling account to the identity theft industry expert who suggested instead of partnering with his company we should partner with his competitor because they were the better fit… and everyone in between. A million thank you's wouldn't be enough. So my job now is to give back whenever and however I can. That's being grateful and the best way to thank those who've helped me immensely.

Believe it will work (like Doc Brown)

Do you remember that awesome 1980's movie Back to the Future? When Doc Brown's time machine finally worked after years of trying, Doc had the most amazing (and amazed) reaction, screaming "IT WORKED! IT WORKED!"

Have you ever had a moment like that? Where after weeks or months or years the thing you were working on finally came together? I call these rare, but defining moments in life "Doc Brown Moments." Doc believed and that's why he succeeded.

If you take that step into the wild, unpredictable, thrilling world of being an entrepreneur, do it for the right reasons…it's not all glitz and glamor. Don't expect a pat on the back or people to think you are special or somehow better. That's not what this is about, you need to do it for YOU. It will be harder than you think, more stressful than you think, require more sacrifice, time, investment, struggle than you think.

But the exhilaration of success, of winning, of defying the odds... experiencing your Doc Brown Moment...it is well worth the blood, sweat, and tears that accompany the journey. Go make your Doc Brown Moment...I promise you'll be glad you did.

I wish you well on your journey!

CHAPTER 4

YOUNG INVENTORS CHANGE THE WORLD EVERY DAY:
Why it's important to raise your children with an entrepreneurial spirit

By **ARNOLD VOLKER**

In 1930 a 16-year-old boy named George Nissen watched a traveling circus and was amazed how the trapeze artists dismounted into a bouncing safety net after their routine. This led him to think about how cool it would be if they could continue to bounce. Imagine what tricks they could perform if instead of just bouncing to land, they bounced back up into the air!

Using his parents' garage, Nissen created a piece of equipment he called a bouncing rig. He simply strapped a canvas sheet to a metal frame. He later added inner tubes between the canvas and the metal frame which eventually became springs. By now you must have figured out what his invention was: the trampoline.

The word "trampoline" came from a Spanish word for diving board: *el trampolin*. He added an e and registered the name "trampoline" as a trademark for the invention. The trampoline eventually became an Olympic sport at the 2000 Sydney Games. Thanks to this young man, millions have enjoyed the fun and exciting experience of bouncing high into the air–something only circus performers could do before.

You'd be surprised how many everyday items in our lives were actually invented by children.

Here's another example: Chester Greenwood invented earmuffs in 1873, at the age of 15. After a cold afternoon of ice skating, he asked his grandmother to sew tufts of warm fur between loops of wire to cover his ears. Greenwood went on to become a manufacturer of ear protectors and also patented many other products, including the tea kettle. His ideas and businesses created jobs for his region of Maine for nearly 60 years.

Okay, one more: in 1905, the 11-year-old Frank Epperson invented the Popsicle. He actually came up with it almost by accident — the story goes that he left a mixture of soda water outside overnight with a stir stick in it, and the mixture froze. He eventually patented the frozen dessert, initially calling it the Epsicle. Over a century later, over two billion Popsicles are consumed every year.

Children are some of the best inventors and innovators in the world. They see things that we adults don't and think of great ideas we'd never come up with–or have already dismissed as too complicated, too simple, or too weird.

If you're reading this book, you probably either already are an entrepreneur or want to become one. But if you have children, or plan on having them, chances are that *they* will want to become entrepreneurs, too! The catch is that they might not know it yet–for kids, entrepreneurship usually looks like coming up with ideas they don't know what to do with.

Your children depend on your ability to lead them. As parents, we have the power to guide and nurture their ideas — or to crush them before they start to grow. *We must not let the second situation happen.* Never disregard or ridicule any of your child's ideas, no matter how complicated, simple, or weird they may seem. Our attitude and faith in our youth will determine not just their destiny, but ours. They are our future, and their small ideas today may stand the test of time like the trampoline, Popsicle, or earmuffs.

When my son Dawson was 12, he came to me and said "Dad, I want a go-kart." I told him that if he wanted one, he'd better figure out how to pay for it. My son has always been a tinkerer, always taking things apart, putting them back together, and trying to come up with new contraptions. So I was confident that he would come up with some way to fund his go-kart, likely by building something totally new and then selling it. Sure enough, a few days later he came back to me with an idea.

A couple of weeks earlier, I had brought home some scrap metal cutouts from work for my son to mess around with. We live in a rural area where 4-H and shooting sports are popular, so it didn't surprise me that Dawson started out using these cutouts as shooting targets — first with a Nerf gun in his bedroom, then outside with a BB gun and a .22 rifle.

You might have guessed what my son's idea was: to use these scrap cutouts to make shooting targets for kids. The cutouts made a satisfying *ting* sound when you shot them, and they also spun around when the pellet or bullet hit them. These elements built confidence for young shooters, since every hit had a clear effect. Dawson called them "Shoot N Spin Targets," a simple and appealing name that kids would understand right away. Zombies were getting popular in TV and movies, so he also suggested putting zombie-themed images on the targets to make them even more fun to shoot.

To make a long story short, selling these targets more than paid for my son's go-kart, and he had a great time both selling them and learning to build a business around them. And as his dad, I not only got to watch him excel and grow, but I also got to learn some important lessons about supporting child entrepreneurs. Here are a few of them:

Their Confidence And Excitement Are Worth All Your Effort

My son's first sale was to a local bar and restaurant. I helped him practice his sales pitch so many times I could have given it instead and made the sale myself. But I knew letting him do it was more important–and the look of excited surprise on his face when the restaurant owner said yes was worth every minute I'd spent helping him. It didn't matter that the sale was only for $50 — he about tipped over. I never was so proud of him before.

As we approached new people to sell them, Dawson got more and more confidence in explaining how the targets were made, wholesale vs. retail, and the possibility to customize. A couple years later, when he was asked to speak about Shoot N Spin at a national event put on by Pheasants Forever, he not only jumped at the chance, but had the guts to ask the keynote speaker — Theresa Vail, aka Miss Kansas 2013 — to attend his presentation.

Man, I would have never had the confidence to do that when I was his age or maybe even now. To my amazement, she said she would love to — and when she raised a hand during his presentation, he proudly said "Miss Kansas, do you have a question?" Priceless memories.

It's Our Job To Help Them Create Opportunities...

The idea was my son's. Getting that idea out into the world is where I came in. My company makes wind spinners for lawns and gardens, so I was able to help him design and manufacture these targets. The prototypes were a tremendous amount of fun both to make and to shoot!

I also reached out to our local newspaper. People love to support and read about kids' success stories, so I pitched the idea of the local paper writing an article on my son to share the story. On August 10, 2013, my son made the front page of the Bemidji Pioneer. We learned that being above the fold and on the front page was a big deal. I forwarded the article to a bunch of other places including the NRA and Pheasants Forever. The NRA has a youth magazine, and they ran the article. Pheasants Forever, as you read above, asked Dawson to speak at the No Child Left Indoors portion of their National Conference in Madison Wisconsin in 2014.

As this story developed, I never looked at my involvement as bragging. As a parent, I see it as my job to help my kids create opportunities.

...And To Help Them Navigate Obstacles

When you are developing a product, every day is a learning experience. Being there for your children when they want to give up can be what makes parenting so special. It's the most important job there is.

When we approached a local sporting goods store, they agreed to try the targets, but they also wanted a version that was thicker for bigger guns before they would commit to an order. Dawson had no idea how to do that, and I was concerned as well. Just by adding one new element, your product might need a lot of changes. We didn't know a lot about ballistics or how thick the new targets should be or what type of metal we would need. We ended up reaching out to a steel supplier, and they were glad to send us the specs on calibers and how far away you needed to be.

I've already mentioned the Pheasants Forever conference a couple times, but there's one more story about it you need to hear: originally, Dawson was supposed to be one of four boys presenting during his hour of stage time. But a few weeks before, the other three presenters dropped out — suddenly he had to fill the whole hour by himself! Now he was panicking — and it was my job to help him get his head together.

"What's the big deal?" I said. "We have plenty of videos, we will figure this out! What about cutting a tree down and bringing it with and hanging all of our designs on it and buying Nerf guns for people to shoot at them?" Dawson really liked that idea. As we prepared the presentation his panic went away. We brought in our best friend, and he agreed to go on the trip and help and take videos of the presentation of the show.

The drive over was memorable–we had a tree strapped to the roof and the back full of inventory to sell at the show. I still chuckle when I think about how silly we must have looked. But who cares? It was in the moment of having pride in his product and creating an environment for people to interact with it.

Your Support Is The Root Of Their Success

Throughout Dawson's growing up I always supported and challenged his desire to invent things. One night he asked me to come to his room when he was 6 or 7 and he had ropes and pulleys to shut off his light from his bed. "Wow," I said, "that was cool. How about adding something so you could also turn it on? I'll come back in 15 minutes, see what you can figure out."

Supporting your kid's creativity and challenging them to make their idea or project better really inspires them. Of course when I came back, he had added some weights and more special items from his room and it worked like a charm. Which led to many other future adventures like getting the largest magnets we could find off the internet for a perpetual motion machine!

The point is not all ideas work but those ideas develop a foundation for creativity and the desire to succeed. Dawson's one idea of getting into shooting targets led to a 10-year manufacturing agreement and a line of products that has kept our company open through some very challenging economic times.

The great thing about children is they don't have the limiting beliefs most of us adults have. As parents, we need to search for those little ways to support and inspire your kids to dream big and lead change no matter what their age. Be supportive, keep creating, there are no failures, just learning lessons. Supporting kids' ideas at a young age can lead to endless opportunities and out-of-this-world results.

CHAPTER 5

HOW TO START OVER
(AND SUCCEED!)

By **CHARLES CHRISTOPHER TYRRELL**

In March of 2020, my life was dealt several blows. I was at a crossroads and had two choices: stay in my current path, or start over. I chose to start over. Over the next several months, I learned many important lessons. I also realized that many of my clients also made decisions to start over, by choosing to leave their country and start over in the United States.

Those who start over and succeed typically follow the same path. Knowing these lessons may help you when you decide to start over. I will share five of these lessons with you in this chapter.

Stick with what you know

You may want to try something new when you start over. Although you may be excited by this shift, this might not be the best idea. I know because I have experienced this first-hand.

In 2016, I decided to start a new business helping others develop systems for businesses to make them more efficient. I had started doing this with my old law firm and felt competent doing it, but it was still relatively new to me, and the business struggled. So in March of 2020, I had the choice of either focusing on developing another new business or starting my own immigration firm, which I had been doing for over ten years. I chose to start the new immigration firm and have found success.

Many of my clients have used their entrepreneurial skills to start a new business in the US. Many of those who not only succeeded in their business ventures, but were also able to use their business to obtain permanent residency in the US, started businesses that were similar to those they ran in their home country.

For example, one client sold various motor vehicle parts and accessories in their home country. This client decided to expand their business into the US, which allowed them to use many of the same contacts to import and export motor vehicle parts. After getting an investor visa for the client, the client expanded the US operations to get close to one million USD in sales, and eventually obtained residency in the US. This was all because the client knew the business before starting his US operations.

Other successful clients had restaurants in their home country and the US, invested in real estate in both countries, or had engineering businesses in both countries. One client was an electrical engineer who purchased and successfully ran an electrical repair business.

However, those clients that chose a different field than they had worked in before coming to the US often struggled.

One of my clients owned a successful pharmacy in a South American country, but when he came to the US he tried to start a haircutting business that specialized in serving children. This business didn't do well — not because he wasn't good at cutting hair or didn't work hard enough, but because his new business ran on a completely different model than his old one.

With South American pharmacies, most customers go to the one closest to their home, going for convenience rather than service. The business in the US, haircuts for children, was entirely reliant upon customer service, something my client wasn't used to focusing on. Although he worked hard in that business, it never worked out and the client made the difficult decision to close it and return to South America.

Looking at my and my clients' struggles, I realize that sticking with what you know gives you the best chance of success. Don't try to re-invent the wheel. You are successful in one area. Take that success and expand upon it, by staying in a similar field. This will give you the best opportunity to succeed.

Believe in yourself

For years, I wanted validation from others. I had placed my identity in how others viewed me, which often had me doing things I didn't necessarily want to do. This was because I lacked self-confidence. So, my first step in March of 2020 was to try and work with a new partner. I wanted someone to validate my decisions. However, this partnership did not succeed and I became frustrated. I then realized I didn't need someone's validation. I just needed to believe in myself.

We all want validation. We all want to know that people appreciate what we do. I love hearing people tell me that I have helped them or that I am wise. I want the praise, but I no longer need it. What I need is to be true to myself.

This is true for business. As entrepreneurs, we need to make decisions that are true to us and the business. Trying to please others may cost us money in many ways, such as employing people who shouldn't be working with us. We have to make smart decisions because our businesses succeed based on what we decide. Waiting for others to validate our decisions only holds us back.

We should seek help from others and get their advice, but the decision should rest with us. Too often I hear of stories from clients who want to change their immigration plan because a friend, neighbor, or family member did something different when they came to the US. What they don't realize is that this person only knows their own experiencel — and that experience might not have been the most efficient or cost-effective way to come to the US.

For example, I helped a client in the beginning of 2021 obtain a work visa for the US. Later in the year, she contacted me to ask about changing her visa. I asked her why and she told me she wanted to follow her father's immigration steps and do what he had done when he came to the US. I advised her that following her father's steps would only delay her plans and cost her more money. She ultimately chose to follow my suggestions, even though it meant losing some validation from her father, and she is now working in the US. If she had followed her father's plan, she would have added several years to her immigration process.

Validation is nice, but it is not necessary. We all have it within ourselves to succeed. We just need to believe it. Realizing that you can do it on your own is one of the most important steps to becoming successful.

Take responsibility

I have read many books by successful business owners. Almost all of these leaders advise that we should take responsibility for everything that happens to us. This means regardless of what happens in life, either good or bad, you are the one who is responsible for what happened. I didn't want to accept this but eventually realized the truth of the sentiment.

A few years ago, a visa request I filed for a client was denied. I reviewed the file and believed I had done everything I could to get an approval. When the client's wife asked me about what happened, I defended my actions and blamed everything on the officer. After speaking with her for over an hour, the client's wife left angry. I realize that my actions likely cost my old firm a lot of business, as she had many friends who could have retained us. I lost her trust and her referrals, all because I didn't take responsibility.

Today, I am learning to take responsibility for all actions. Recently, I was working on an online form and typed in the name of the company, which the program autocorrected to another name. I sent the proposed form to a representative of the company and several other individuals. None of us caught the typo and I submitted the request. Six months later, when we got the form certified, a company representative noticed the typo. As I was the one who typed in the information, I took full responsibility and agreed to start the process over again. I did not charge the client for this additional work, explaining that I made the mistake. All parties understood and I not only was allowed to complete the work, but have received some referrals from this process.

Taking responsibility is hard. We have to acknowledge our mistakes when our natural reaction is to blame someone else. However, when we take responsibility for everything that happens in our life, we actually show strength and character, and others recognize this resolve. People appreciate it when you accept responsibility.

Don't be afraid to fail

For most of my life, I was afraid to fail. I feared rejection which cost me dates. I was afraid to try new things, for fear that I wouldn't do it right. I was afraid that if I failed, it meant that I wasn't the best person I could be.

The fear of failure holds most of us back. It may often hold us back in making decisions. We need to make quick decisions, test them, and pivot when they don't work. When we don't, we lose out on opportunities and are held back in life rather than achieve the success we know is within us.

One of the ways that I have seen the fear of failure hold us back is by saying we need more information before we make a decision. We all need some information, but shouldn't use gathering information to hold us back. I have had many clients ask for more information only to delay making a decision. This has often cost them many opportunities.

Several years ago, an immigration benefit was set to expire for a group of people. My team and I had many clients that were affected by this and we provided them with all the information they needed to make a decision to proceed and obtain the immigration benefit. Unfortunately, many of these clients failed to make a decision and some of them had no other immigration options. Their fear of failure severely impacted their lives.

Failure is good because it is often our best teacher. We learn more when we fail than we ever do when we succeed. When we fail, we know that we need to change something. In fact, most of the successful people in the world failed time and time again. Think about Thomas Edison. He had countless failures before he had success. I've even heard that 7-Up is called 7-Up because the inventor failed six previous times before he found the formula that is now 7-Up. It is the failures that lead to ultimate success.

Don't give up

The last lesson that I want to impart is don't give up. The only way you are guaranteed to not succeed is if you quit. As long as you continue to learn and move forward, you will eventually reach success.

With every business venture, there are going to be times when it looks as though there is no hope. You may be looking at your business right now and wondering how it's going to survive. That's the position one of my clients was in about a year ago. She had started borrowing money just to stay afloat and was considering returning to her home country. Listening to her story and her struggles, I told her that every successful person I'd ever met or read about had come to a similar situation. The successful ones chose to persevere and shortly after things turned around. My client thanked me and shortly thereafter, her business did turn around. She got her visa, her business became a success, all because she didn't quit when things looked hopeless.

We all come to points where we want to quit. I have had these thoughts as well. However, I looked at the bigger picture and continued to move forward. I have broken through and continue to move forward to my lofty goals. I am succeeding and I know you can too.

Conclusion

Starting over is hard. It takes courage and dedication. However, if you continue at it, you will succeed. Every successful person had to start from the bottom. They all had to make the same decisions you did and they succeeded by following the above rules. You can do this. You have it in you. Don't give up. You will succeed. I've seen it countless times with my clients and by applying these lessons in my own life, I am successful. I know you will be successful as well.

CHAPTER 6

DO THE RIGHT THING, AT THE RIGHT TIME, FOR THE RIGHT REASONS

By **DEMETRA BAKAS**

"Find a job you love and never work a day in your life." This is a common saying that many of us strive for, and I can confidently and humbly say that I have a job I love and can help you find yours too. This isn't a message about perfection, the easy route, or a privileged opportunity. This is what happened to me, under no special circumstances or upbringing. My hope is that it inspires you.

In my first year out of college, I was offered an exciting opportunity to be an executive recruiter at one of the largest global recruiting firms in the world. I was enticed by the company's lucrative compensation potential, growth opportunities, plentiful resources, and large support network. Did I mention the free lunches, happy hours, cool swag, and company-sponsored trips?

I remember it like it was yesterday. I walked up to a high-rise building in the city excited to start this new chapter. I landed on the 70th floor only to see beautiful glass double doors with the company's lit-up name shining behind them. I was excited by this proud feeling of "I made it!"

Little did I know, it was all a façade.

At my fingertips was an opportunity to make a lot of money and reach my life goals to help my family and build a life for myself. But there was a catch. I had to speak and act in a way that isn't my true identity. I was supposed to mimic my superiors although their methodology did not align with how I wanted to conduct business. I was asked to do whatever it took to meet my daily metrics and annual gross profit quota, no matter who I had to run over.

This is what I was told time and time again. According to Google statistics, I am 1 of 227,827 recruiters in the United States. Being a $23B industry, one can only imagine the pressure I felt as a driven individual in a highly competitive industry.

Let's do some simple math. Now, imagine what you could do with $30,000. What if I told you you could earn this amount in a single transaction by simply doing the right thing, at the right time, for the right reasonsl — without falling victim to the possibly unethical and demoralizing methods I shared earlier?

In direct hire recruiting, you earn a commission when you successfully match a qualified candidate to a client's job opening. It is calculated by multiplying the placement fee percentage by the candidate's first-year base salary. (To debunk the ever-popular myth, the fee does not come out of a candidate's base salary!) The earned commission is split up into four equal parts based on candidate and client ownership. In this $30,000 example, each piece of the pie is worth $7,500 so you have the opportunity of earning 1 slice up to all 4 slices of the deal.

In order to stand behind our work, we offer assurances to companies in the rare chance a candidate does not perform well or remain employed through the guarantee period. Although our goal is for this beautiful matchmaking to last forever, things happen out of our control that ultimately kill the deal.

It is hard, annoying, and no one likes to do it. But when a deal falls apart and you lose your hard-earned commission, it is easy to walk away from a client because there are thousands of others to choose from. And this is just one example where a shifted mindset to doing the right thing, at the right time, for the right reasons will lead you ahead of your competition.

Do The Right Thing

Doing the right thing is what I believe has led me to success in all aspects of my personal and professional life. Sounds simple, but it takes a conscious effort to stay in this lane for some, whereas it is second nature for others. The catalyst in accomplishing this is by going about your business in the right way as a genuine, honest, and trustworthy individual.

Genuine in how you express your feelings, honest in how you articulate information, and trustworthy in how you manage relationships. These are what I believe are imperative character traits in order to be a good leader and to influence your followers. The more integrity you have in your work, the more others will trust you, the more they want to work with you again, the more business they refer to you, and more importantly, the better you sleep at night.

When I say I have a job I love, I mean it. Being able to impact lives, drive businesses forward, make meaningful relationships is just a day in the life of a recruiter. Who else can say that their goal at work every day is to make friends?

While its lucrative commission potential is uncapped, more importantly, it is an industry where you can literally make a difference in peoples' lives. It is the reason I have continued to never give up and pursue my passion in helping professionals reach their ultimate career goals.

Oftentimes in the matchmaking process, I am presented with two options – right or wrong. Recently I was assisting my candidate, let's call him Bill, a top-tier accounting candidate, who was looking to transition into the next chapter of his career. As most candidates do, he explored a variety of opportunities and landed himself three job offers–one with my client and two with peer recruiters. Undeniably, each recruiter would prefer for him to accept their offer to earn a commission. However, the right thing to do is give the candidate space to decide which opportunity is best for them without the biased opinion of a recruiter.

Simply put, a recruiter, or headhunter as some like to call us, has a reputation of acting solely based on the motivating factor of money. And that is where I think differently. The best compliment I receive is when my unbiased, transparent, and "keep it real" attitude is appreciated. Even if it doesn't seal the deal at that moment.

Because I always lead with this mindset, I feel fulfilled. Surely, it is not possible for me to place every single person I talk to, or fill every opening my clients trust me with, but if I can help you update your resume, create your career game plan, prep you for an interview, share market intel, or refer you to my network, then I feel it is equally rewarding.

In that situation with Bill, he appreciated my genuine approach and asked me in confidence as his trusted advisor for my opinion on which opportunity is best for his career. Those two roads flashing in front of me again! — I could use my power of influence to lead him down my road so I become $30,000 richer. Or I could lead with my moral compass and fairly display the facts of the job opportunity and admit that perhaps my client does not offer everything he is looking for. I guarantee you in situations like these, the right thing to do is to be genuine, honest, and trustworthy.

...at the right time...

I assume you have heard the phrase "timing is everything" or "time is of the essence." (Unfortunately for me, I am on "Greek time" so I am always 10 minutes late.)

However, in the sales world, we say "time kills all deals."

In the beginning of my career, I never thought I would switch recruiting firms, let alone *start* my own firm one day. Since we are bound by non-confidentiality and non-solicitation agreements, it can be very scary, financially burdensome, and difficult to make a move since you have to start from scratch again.

For years, I had built my book of business, worked on numerous searches, and learned through a lot of trial and error. I gained knowledge and experience but also struggled. A LOT. I busted my butt, cold-called more times than I can remember, and made more mistakes than I can forget. A lot of those first voicemails I left were awful! I survived a great amount of adversity which included 14-hour hustle days, sneaky coworkers, impossible client demands, and extreme competition. There were many times where I told myself, "I can't do this."

Even through all the struggle, I am most proud of myself for maintaining my moral compass, which resulted in me rightfully earning my spot as a top biller. Throughout the years, I learned to trust my gut and gain a level of confidence in what I do and how I do it. When speaking with clients and candidates, I proved my commitment to them by being neutral and transparent which always wins regardless of the outcome.

The way to do that is…

Confidence.

Build it. Test it. Realize it.

When I left my first recruiting firm for a competitor, I didn't even meet the team before accepting the new job. Crazy, right? To me, it didn't matter, nor did the noisy behavior of others. It was because I had built my confidence in knowing I could close a deal from start to finish no matter my surroundings or resources. Because I hustled and always followed my moral compass, things would fall into place at the right time. I would recruit a candidate and magically their dream job would fall into my lap. I would gain a new client with a difficult search and magically my network would refer me to the best-suited candidate.

I repeat – timing is everything. Had I never left company A for company B, I would have never imagined myself at the peak of my career today. Fortunately, those moves are what introduced me to my future business partners which platformed me to launch my own boutique recruiting firm from the ground up. Everything fell into place as my belief in myself grew and the right timing presented itself.

...for the right reasons

As an executive recruiter, my job is to match top finance and accounting talent with industry-leading workplaces. In its best light, it can be full of relationship building, matchmaking, and problem-solving. However, like most sales jobs, the industry is quite cut-throat, which caused me to learn many serious lessons very early on.

From stealing commissions to sabotaging candidates to misrepresenting job opportunities, I have experienced and witnessed many situations where things were done for the wrong reasons by those around me. I have seen it over and over again – money makes people do funny things. And by funny, I mean, out of character, without integrity, and for an easy buck.

Remember my candidate Bill?

He decided to accept another job offer that served as a better strategic move for him in his career. And guess what? I was genuinely thrilled for him. While declining my offer was not ideal for me, it was the best decision for him. As a matter of fact, it paid tenfold when he referred me to two other candidates earning me 2X the commission, and more importantly, a solid reputation due to my honest approach with him because I genuinely care.

In business, you are never doing it for the right reasons if it's for quick profits over people. You have to have the other person's welfare in mind. As I have grown into my success over the years, the common thread has always been a personal, not financial, approach. While the wrong thing can sometimes be enticing, in the long run, leading with the right reasons will pay off in more ways than you can imagine.

Call it karma, call it coincidence, but I believe acting for the right reasons allows you to have a clear conscience and have the pressure taken off of you to potentially act wrongfully. And in my recruiting experience, it has always amounted to greater profits than those around me who do not lead with the right reasons mindset.

Put it all together!

It is easy to assume that when someone reaches a certain level of success that it was handed to them on a silver platter. But, I am nothing special. I grew up in an immigrant family where I was the first to graduate with a college degree. I worked endless hours to find a spot in an industry that I didn't even know had space for me. It is my experience and my values that have led me to believe that anyone can find success.

Of course, you don't have to be a recruiter to follow this, although we are always looking for like-minded people who are passionate about our industry. If you bring this motto to your work, you will find success. It may take time, it may be challenging, and it may not look exactly the way you think at first, but I guarantee you, if you do the right thing at the right time for the right reasons, you will be successful before long.

As a reminder, not everyone's entrepreneurial journey has necessarily been easy. I have experienced a couple of failed partnerships, botched business ideas, mismatched candidate placements, and a rollercoaster of highs and lows. I persevered and realized that if I invest in myself and focus on my mission, then I can continue to achieve greatness.

I say this humbly and truthfully! — I can't attribute my success as a lone ranger either. I have great mentors, business partners, and colleagues that I met along the way that have always given me that "kick in the butt" motivation to keep going.

Thanks to this wild ride, I am now the founding partner of a boutique finance and accounting recruiting firm specializing in direct-hire placement. I strategically recruit staff to senior leadership candidates for clients ranging from high-growth start-ups to Fortune 500 companies in a variety of industries specifically in the areas of corporate accounting, internal audit, corporate tax, financial reporting, and financial planning and analysis.

My goal is to share my story and have it impact those who are unsure of themselves, just like I was. If I can spark your interest in launching your next entrepreneurial idea or finding your next career opportunity, it would give me the motivation to keep doing what I am doing. You see, it doesn't matter where you come from or where you started, it matters most where you end up – *by doing the right thing, at the right time, for the right reasons.*

CHAPTER 7

TAKE THE SHOT

By **DEREK GERBER**

It's easy to understand what it means to take your shot. You've probably got an idea right now of a shot you could take in your professional or personal life. Maybe you've already taken several.

What's harder is to know how to take your shot in the way that is most likely to lead to success. In this chapter, I'll share with you six steps I've found helpful in taking successful shots.

Step 1: Define success

The first step to taking your shot is defining your vision of success. In other words, you've got to know where the basket is before you can shoot the ball. Is your metric a certain amount of money, a specific sales goal, or a company you'd like to work for? Or is it happiness or pride or a certain lifestyle, something that can't easily be measured by a number on a page? These are all very different examples of what others might determine as success.

I know people who don't make six figures but are very happy traveling the world without any cares. That's their life vision, and no one can take that away from them. Nobody would be able to persuade them otherwise or say that they aren't a success just because they haven't reached incredible financial heights or some title in a company.

Defining success is even more important than ever in our fast-changing world. New technologies and global events are rapidly evolving and seemingly have the power to quickly alter society, for better and for worse. How are these events going to change your views on life and in your career? Will the things you can't control, control your view on success? Do you want money, flexibility, experiences, and/or all of the above?

Start with the bigger picture of where you are now, and then work it backwards from there to picture yourself one year, three years, and five years from this point in time. Now, take the shot on commiting yourself to this dream in the next step.

Step 2: Do research

Once you know which metric you want to use to measure success, you have to figure out a goal that's both challenging and realistic. Dreaming is different that pursuing a dream.

One of the biggest mistakes I see people make is setting goals without really thinking through the work it takes to hit them. I'm sure that nearly every person would love to make a million dollars a year, but how many have sat down and divided a million by twelve? That's a lot more money per month than many people realize, and that revelation is step one. We haven't even considered the time, effort, or sacrifices yet. It's just to simplify what that number means over the year. Your goals might have different baselines.

In this example, we are picking a large salary or sales quota number. When you've got that number down, you need to put more math around it. How many products do you need to sell? How much can you spend on expenses if you're bringing in that kind of revenue? How does your pricing impact these targets? How much time can you realistically put into your work, versus the capacity to deliver?

Maybe your goals aren't financial, but instead are focused on life satisfaction. If your goal is to travel the world, that still takes planning. How much will the trip cost? Have you spoken to other people who have gone where you want to go? Are you following travel blogs about your intended destinations? You need to put energy into figuring out whether your travel goals are realistic and worthy before you start pursuing them. Document your research and next step tasks along the way with dates to keep you on track.

To answer these questions about business and life, you have to do your research. Some sorts of research are easier than ever, like a Google search. Yet, often, finding the answers you really need comes down to a tried-and-true source of wisdom: your networks. Write down your ideas and make them make sense, but then go out and find people who will give you some other ideas around yours in a community that supports your vision. You'll find that there are actually more people willing to give advice or input than you previously may have thought. The challenge is really more about picking apart which pieces of advice work best for you in your situation.

I go to LinkedIn to find similar peers I can reach out to for whatever I need. I get a response most of the time, and I've built many healthy business relationships that way. If you're in a different industry, the platform for finding your peers may be different as well. There are so many new platforms coming out right now – perhaps emerging platforms such as Discord, Clubhouse, or even TikTok are where you're going to find the right people to get started with refining your vision.

No matter where your network is, don't be afraid to get in touch and scratch their brains a bit. You can read all the books you want to generate ideas and learn techniques, but the feedback on those ideas from peers is impossible to replicate.

Step 3: Take action

After you've defined your measure of success and done your research to generate a quality strategy for self-accountability, the next step to taking your shot is putting the plan into action. It's no longer the time to just talk or think about your vision as now you have to pull it off. You've already got the goal and your first action steps scheduled, so now execute the plan.

Taking your shot is 50% science, and 50% art form. The science is the networking, the number crunching, and the information gathering. The art is all up to you. You have to decide for yourself how you want to market and brand yourself to the world in your own way.

I've seen lots of great ideas never come to life because there were no next steps taken in a plan. Put the plan in that makes your idea come to life. Sometimes the first steps are simple, but then can get more complex later.

When you're struggling with this part of planning, it's helpful to seek our mentors and valued peers for their input. Most of the time, you'll realize that you have the capacity to take the right steps on your own. However, I do recommend that you seek out others who can guide you along the way so that you can consistently stay on track. Too many people start with a great idea, take a few steps, and then seemingly lose interest which is where a mentor or leadership group can really push you towards greater accountability.

At the end of the day, you don't need to have all of the answers to continue down this pathway to success because plans and information evolve over time. You must love the journey and the grind along the way. Mentors help provide new perspectives and input you may not have considered as you were busy focusing on other elements.

I was fortunate enough to have some more experienced people watching over me through the years as I developed my business identity. From there, I provided my own style and forged my own brand through the art of doing things the way I learned from the first hand experiences that I gained.

Step 4: Avoid shortcuts

There's no shortcut to success when you want to do things the right way. Make the plan, do the research, and schedule your tasks. Those steps are all easier than committing yourself to these goals every single day. Step 4 is truly about staying consistent in your grind to greatness. Get better every day and measure your results. Use data to drive your focus on getting results so you can stay constructive in the process.

One of the greatest lessons I learned from working with my dad was to keep everything "above the table." There's a right way of treating people, and a right way of doing business. It starts and ends with integrity. Keeping things simple and transparent with yourself and others is more important than anything. Commit to consistence on executing your plan, yet don't forget to stop and enjoy the view along the way as you move through your journey.

Step 5: Make adjustments

Every player misses shots. The difference between the average and the successful players is how they make adjustments to get it right the next time. Only perfect practice makes perfect.

It's important to remember that you're looking to share your value, yet also learn from others too. While the business results were always fun for me to chase, it was important to refine parts of my own style and soft skills to become a better leader. Just being excitable and energetic wasn't enough to get results at the next level while pursuing my dreams. I wondered, "Can I truly make a difference and motivate people?" As a young professional, I'll admit that those conversations with myself did give me some insecurities, but they also inspired me to make adjustments while I took my shots.

Once you've put your plan into action, have the humility to accept when to make adjustments. Please take it from me, a person who has always taken results personally, to not put so much pressure on yourself during this process. It's about getting 1% better every day. Overnight successes can take years of hard work and dedication. You'll find on these paths that you may not like where you are headed at times, or perhaps you can't let go of the the type of person you were before. Perhaps you want to travel or start a family, so your idea of success quickly changes with your dreams. Roll with it and live your best life.

Garnering constructive criticism doesn't mean you're a failure. You can come back and try a different way using the feedback you've received, and in all likelihood, it'll work out better than you could've thought. It's all just part of taking the shot. Remember, it's ok to change your mind with new information. It's what smart people do all of the time.

Use the data to make binary decisions, adjust your plan, and keep grinding. The only failure lies within ignoring the data and refusing to grow yourself along the way. True business leaders admit that nobody has it all figured out. Once you give up that idea of perfection, then the road gets a lot more fun along the way. Enjoy the journey.

Step 6: Keep shooting

The wonderful thing about taking the shot is that there's always another one to be taken. At first, you may have to keep refining and repeating the same shot over and over again before you get it right. After that, you can go for a different angle when you look for the next opening. The opportunity I had to transition from software into the video marketing industry didn't come because I was specifically looking for it. It came because I took the first shot and kept following through in the right way, which led to the chance at the next one. The most successful people you know didn't always know the next steps, yet they pushed on anyway.

I played football for 14 years and coached for seven. There's a great saying that's common in the sport: "What have you done for me lately?" It doesn't matter if you worked hard and made great plays a week ago as you have to make the big play in the game today.

That's what keeps the cycle going, onto breaking more records and winning more championships. In business, as in sports, you can't become complacent after making only one successful shot.

Those stories that I shared were invaluable learning opportunities for me as I built up resilience and respect for the process. My father always wanted me to get to the top while starting at the bottom by doing things the right way. I could only achieve what I have accomplished by taking the path less traveled by others. However, the most important thing I have learned along the way is how to take care of people. I'm forever grateful for my mentors and all of the challenges during this journey as they put me years ahead of where I thought I could be on my own.

Part of taking the shot is learning how to get over that failure and move on to the next one. You've got to keep taking your shot. Do the math and you'll figure out that the more shots you take, the sooner you'll find success, happiness, and pure fulfillment in life.

I hope this simple advice gives you the same motivation to embrace the excitement of pursuing your dreams as you carve out your own journey through life too.

CHAPTER 8

FOCUS ON THE PEOPLE

By **DON G. KING**

The biggest lesson in business leadership that I have learned is that if you improve the quality of life of others, then your own life will improve. For me, life and business are interconnected, so this lesson applies both in work and in personal life.

As a leader, it is important that I always serve as a giver. Some people think a leader is someone who holds employees accountable to get them to do what they want. But in my eyes, a leader is the one who is down in the thick of it with the employees and works through issues with them on a day-to-day basis. If we all work to help each other in business, then we have a more cohesive team that can, inevitably, produce better results. A leader is someone who gives people a foot up and helps them improve the quality of their lives.

This is a win-win situation. So when a new employee joins the company, I let them know that I am all about everyone bringing their skills to the table and working to the benefit of the company as a whole. As a result, the company will take care of all of us. It's not me. It's not you. It's collectively all of us as a team. I believe that if you do that enough and pay it forward, it will eventually come back to you. And over the last 40 years, I've found that it does indeed come back to you.

This was something I loved bringing to life as a franchise developer. People would come in who were far smarter than me in a specific area or skill but had never run a business before. So I got to come in, teach them how to scale their business and how the business side of things work and it was extremely gratifying. I was helping to improve their lives and nothing felt better.

Below are five central points I've discovered over the years that will help anyone in any business find success by helping others.

Learn From The Right People

I didn't come to learn the importance of helping others all on my own. I have to thank my mentors and the relationships that I built with them. One of my earliest mentors, Ralph Palmen, helped me through some really tough times, including when a customer had stolen payrolls from us to the point where it could have put me out of business. It was this mentor that taught me to watch out for the ones that say "it's just business." Value those who give you a helping hand because those are the ones that you should continue to do business with and grow with.

This mentor also taught me that when you feel like you're on top of the world with your business, you need to remember the times when you were struggling and reach out a helping hand to bring people up to that mountaintop with you because it's guaranteed that at some point, you'll be back down in that valley again. Life is a series of rollercoasters – there are ups and there are downs. Everyone wants to be in this straight line of euphoric happiness where everything is great all the time, but you and I both know that's not possible.

So instead, it becomes about keeping your head about you when you're struggling and remembering that those good times will come back. But even more than that is making sure that you surround yourself with the right people. If you surround yourself with sharks, then you're swimming with sharks. I believe Patrick Lencioni said it best in his book, *The Ideal Team Player*, when he describes hungry, humble, and smart people. If you can make that your focus and hire people with that mindset, it will help everybody move in a positive direction.

Hire the Right People

How do I choose the right people? First, I take the time to really profile the executives that I'm going to do business with. It's much easier today than it used to be. LinkedIn, Facebook, and more can give you a good idea of someone's character based on what they post and who they associate with. I don't know it all, but what I do know is people, and I know how to put teams of people together that are going to move forward towards a better direction for the entire organization.

That starts with choosing to hire people who truly want to grow and who are willing to do the work to get there. Remember Patrick Lencioni's big three: hungry, humble, and smart. Do they want to learn? Are they hungry to grow? Are they humble enough to engage in training and take advice from others? Are they smart enough to learn quickly and not make the same mistakes over and over again?

Someone may not have all three, but if they're smart and humble, then I can teach them how to be hungry. However, if you're not humble, that's usually a deal-breaker for us.

Keep the Right People

Part of the challenge is finding people, but the next challenge comes in keeping them. It is up to the employer to provide an environment that is somewhere the employee wants to be. Because if it's not, then they'll just go somewhere else. People place so much emphasis on raising the minimum wage which is important, but not the most important thing. The first is to respect people. People don't quit companies, they quit people.

It is a major problem in the modern world how many people do not experience the respect that they deserve to have in the workplace. This includes colleagues, but most importantly, this lack of respect seems to come from their employers. Too many managers, employers, and companies as a whole today see people as just a number rather than actual people.

The most important connection in the organization is who you're directly reporting to. If that person doesn't respect you and simply tells you what to do, then they will burn you out. That either leads to you quitting, or you developing resentment. And neither of those paths are ones anyone wants to take.

Teaching people how to communicate and engage with others is a driving factor in retention in an organization. Human capital is the greatest asset in any organization, bar none. It doesn't matter if a company pays its employees more, has better benefits, etc. What matters is how much the company engages its employees, which, in the bigger picture, translates to how much the company respects its employees.

Challenge Your People

No one wants to live a life that doesn't include any growth. And that means that no one wants to be in a company where they don't experience growth that helps them grow in other areas of their life. Thus, it's important to place emphasis on challenging your employees and providing them with the opportunity to grow.

My primary role as CEO is focusing on strategic growth initiatives for the company, but also influencing team relationships where we are going to get these next big clients that fit our cultural mold. Everyone is always recruiting in our business and it's important to acknowledge that sales is everyone's responsibility in a company.

Say, for example, that you're a CPA trying to start a CPA firm and you're a left-brained analytical person. You still have to have the aptitude of human engagement, which is all sales. Sales aptitude doesn't mean salesman. You don't have to be a sales guru but you have to be able to communicate and engage with people. And, to me, the people that have the best engagement and communication skills make the best salespeople. It's the part about getting over the fear of engaging with new people that is the most difficult.

If you find people with good communication skills and who have a good core value of helping others, you can lead them to the right place and they will run with it. And beyond that, I want people who will challenge themselves and the company. I want people who will come up with new ideas.

Reward Your People The Right Way

So many companies simply shove human capital down to the HR department and it's the expected responsibility of this department to make sure that the company has morals and culture for the employees to align with. Leadership workshops, people workshops, and pizza parties are great. But they're not enough.

There needs to be more of an incentive than just morals, culture, and money. Instead, the entire company needs to revolve around human capital and rewarding people for the work that they do. If you have someone who is recognition-oriented, then you need to be providing them recognition when they are successful in their job. If they're not recognition-oriented, then you need to find another way to reward them. Being recognized at least by your boss for doing a good job goes much further than anyone gives it credit.

In my opinion, a reward shouldn't be a plaque or award with their name on it but instead something bigger like donating to a charity in their name and giving them a certificate. That will take you 100 miles further than a plaque, because you're doing something they care about now, and something you care about. And, you're helping others. This ties back into my whole idea of how the most successful companies are the ones that love their people.

Love Your People

It is important as the leader of a business to focus efforts on the production side of your business and ensure that processes are being followed. That's essential. However, the problem lies in the fact that leaders put *too* much energy into this and lose the importance of the people.

Now, this sounds like something that may just deem those types of leaders selfish people, but they are actually doing themselves a great deal of harm by not giving their people the attention they need. Without love, respect, challenge, help, and support, employees will have no interest in loving, respecting, challenging, helping, and supporting your business. Money may be enough to get an employee, but it is not enough to keep them.

Thus, take the time, put in the effort to find the right people, reward the right people, keep the right people, and love the right people. Without that, you have nothing. There are plenty of other things that matter in creating a successful business, but at the root of everything is people.

CHAPTER 9

FROM BROKEN SYSTEM TO BRIGHT FUTURE:

The Mental Health Revolution We Need Is Already Starting

By **G COLE**

It's the worst kept secret in the medical community: Our country's mental health system is broken. From 2014 to 2020, the number of U.S. adults experiencing depression skyrocketed by 150%, according to Census Bureau data. That's from a survey taken in the very beginning of the pandemic, before we knew it would restrict our ability to connect with others and carry out our normal functions without fear of infection for over a year and half.

Most of our mental health care providers are well-meaning. It's made up of doctors who do as they've been taught by the medical establishment, relying on systems and traditions that are clearly not working given that anxiety and depression rates are headed in the completely wrong direction. The big pharmaceutical companies certainly don't object to the culture of indiscriminate prescription of chemical balancers, and in fact often promote it as a part of a doctor's education.

The main problem I see in today's mental health treatment, the one I've devoted the last 20 years of my life to solving, is that the industry separates the body and mind from each other. What we think of as the mind is housed in our nervous system, the connections throughout our body that sense and feel. In other words, the mind lives in electrical currents created in our bodies. So nothing is ever "just in your mind" – every thought you have becomes part of your body.

We seem to recognize this connection in areas of neuroscience not directly tied into mental health, like learning. For example, if you go to a rock climbing class and are shown some techniques, we know you're going to mentally commit to trying the techniques and then actually perform them using your body. Now, you're creating neural pathways for rock climbing. When you go to sleep and dream that night, you'll solidify the learning into your subconscious and those pathways will start sending signals to the rest of your body. Your pulmonary system may rewire so that your lungs have more air capacity for climbing, or your digestive system may slightly change the way it breaks down food to give you more energy.

The medical establishment has some interesting answers for the mental health crisis in our country. For example, many government agencies claim that about half the population is resistant to traditional treatment, be it pharmaceuticals or talk therapy. This framing of "treatment-resistant" patients and mental illnesses allows those running the industry to throw their hands up and say, "Well, we have the solutions for people, but they just won't accept them!" At the same time, it's a glaring admission that their solutions don't work as well as they should. If the treatment doesn't work for half of the people you're trying to help, why not adjust the treatment to fit the population rather than cast them off?

The root of the system's failures

To figure out how to fix our treatments, we have to realize what is at the root of their failures. It goes back to the fact that most providers are only looking to produce results for half of the mental health equation: just the mind and not the body. It's certainly no coincidence that this medical mindset produces treatments that are only effective for half the population.

This isn't all the fault of the profession — they simply aren't equipped with the necessary tools to make better choices for their patients. When you go see a doctor for a purely physical ailment, there are dozens of objective, measurable tests they'll likely perform on you right away. They'll know exactly what to prescribe you based on your age, weight, blood pressure, lung capacity, and other vitals. These same doctors will tell you that "mindset" is extremely important, yet they do not have tests to determine how helpful or detrimental your mindset is.

Worse than that, if your mindset is detrimental to your healing, they do not have an effective way to help you heal that mindset. It is even worse if you come to your doctor and tell them you're depressed. They are not able to find out what's really going on in your physical brain; instead, they just make assumptions based on what may have worked for patients who came in with similar complaints. Their typical treatment plan is to try out various medications to see "If it works."

These ill-advised prescriptions make up a large part of the system's ineffective treatments. For example, doctors will often recommend a drug like Prozac, a selective serotonin reuptake inhibitor (SSRI), for depression. If the problem is chemical imbalances, wouldn't it make sense to measure the amount of serotonin in someone's brain before trying to solve the issue with something that will affect their level of serotonin? Most doctors make no such effort. You'll go to your primary care physician, tell them you're feeling depressed, and they'll prescribe you an SSRI because that's what's traditionally prescribed by the medical industry.

So it's not surprising that SSRIs like Prozac only work on about 25% of patients they are prescribed to. There's no objective measurement of your mental state, only the doctor's subjective evaluation. Even if they recommend you to a psychiatrist, is that recommendation based on any objective, scientific analysis of your brain's needs? No, it's all dependent on information gained from the subjective point of view of other peoples' personal experiences and word of mouth.

A better way

There has to be a better way of treating mental health, one that connects the mind and body and really gets to the root of the issue. That's what I knew when I founded Pathwaves, a digital therapeutics company. Before I tell you about our work, you should know about our philosophy, one that I believe can be applied by anyone in the mental health industry as well as the entire medical industry to improve medicine and mental health for all of us.

One of the biggest obstacles to our mental health is that something I call our "animal instincts" are overactive. Long ago, when humans lived mostly in tribes and fought every day for their survival, most of our instincts were tuned by fear. A fear-based mindset made sense back then — danger was always lurking around the corner, and sticking out from the tribe could get you killed. Our society has advanced to meet most of our material survival needs, yet many of us still have the same fearful nervous system.

In the modern day, this evolutionary fearfulness is the underlying cause of so much anxiety and wasted mental energy. What other people think about us very rarely affects our chances of survival, but our nervous system still gets half of its signaling from those inputs. We need our minds and bodies to catch up with the societal progress around us. We need to reach a higher level of humanity, one based on love rather than fear.

That's the approach we've built into Pathwaves, and the data clearly supports our method over traditional mental health treatments. In a clinical trial with over 132 participants, 100% saw improved mental health. The average improvement for anxiety was 64%, and the average improvement for depression was 54%. Nine out of ten also reported better sleep, with an average improvement rate of 63%. How do we do it? Put simply, we nurture our love-based instincts and use an innovative understanding of the connection between mind and body.

The Pathwaves method

The first thing Pathwaves does with a patient is conduct a mind scan, also known as a qEEG, which maps the connections between the mind and body. From this, we can identify practically all of the common issues: identity performance, anxiety, physical pain, addiction, excess worry, phobias, anger, and sleep and focus troubles. Traditionally, a diagnosis of one of these would lead straight to treatment, but we opted for a more holistic approach instead. We take all of this data and put it into a numerical scale – a thermometer of the mind, if you will. Where a patient lands on that scale determines what sort of treatment we give them and how much. Typically we give ten sessions of "Neuro Empowerment," which is designed to teach people sustainable, lifelong mind (and body) skills they can use to improve their mental health.

In Neuro Empowerment, the patient wears a pair of earphones plus electrode sensors that take thousands of brain wave measurements every second. We track each frequency band of electricity, assign each frequency band a digital sound tone, and playback (using headphones or speakers) live-time the pattern that the patient's nervous system is creating. It's the music of your mind, played back to you in real time. In the first session, we play back your brain pattern in sonic form, then adjust the sound to whatever trait we are trying to shape in the mind. If we are working to show your mind how to reduce anxiety, we calculate the tones of 50% calm, then play 10% calmer, and so on until you hear complete calmness and your mind responds.

Why does it work? It's all about mirror neurons, one component of the animal instincts that is still immensely useful. The basic idea is that when we see someone do something, our brain understands what they did and connects the neurons needed to mimic the action ourselves. Instead of copying another person, the audio-response therapy helps us copy the brain wave signals necessary to achieve certain mental states. Just like with the rock climbing example I mentioned earlier, patients are building up neurons that will be reinforced through sleep and subconscious practice, only this time they'll be using them to climb out of their mental health struggles. For many, that's the biggest mountain to conquer of all.

Effective application of this strategy is not limited to audio exercises. With some patients, we'll help develop mantra-based routines. For example, a series of repeated phrases and visualizations helped a recent patient feel like his inner child was safe enough for him to be able to sleep. Now that he knows the routine, he can do it for the rest of his life and sleep well nearly every night, in contrast to him being dependent on some kind of medication for sleep.

For others, we may have them watch a screen with colors that correspond to different neural pathways. The nervous system learns which patterns go with their desired state of mind almost immediately, and we then work with the patients on replicating their desired visual patterns when they're away from the screen. Whether it's visual, auditory, or aural stimuli, the patient now knows that they can rewire their brain to stay calmer in the future.

Revolutionizing mental health care

To truly revolutionize mental health care, we have to make it more accessible than just to people who have the time to come to sessions and trainings. That's why I'm a huge proponent of wearable mental health technology. We are all familiar with smart devices that measure all aspects of our physical lives – from how many steps we take to how quickly our heart beats to how many calories we burn. What if we had the same approach for mental health? I truly believe it would revolutionize the mental health of our society, and I'm so excited for the technology to get there that I've invested in it myself.

Imagine what a mental health wearable would look like if it were implemented in the military, a segment of society where peoples' mental health is often tragically overlooked to the point of developing post-traumatic stress disorder. Soldiers or pilots could wear a cap liner with neural sensors in it and speakers or earbuds on the side. A mental health professional would be able to detect when a service member is feeling depression or anxiety, or even just a flashing moment of panic, and in real time offer an intervention to help them calm down. It would not only help them get through the immediate situation without losing their cool, but also help prevent their body from storing trauma in the long term.

I've got a lot of big ideas, but I know I can't do it alone. We need brave doctors, scientists, and entrepreneurs everywhere to stand up to the mental health establishment and demand change to a system that's not working. The practices in place disconnect the body and mind, leaving our outdated animal instincts in control of our lives and our world divided into tribes. What if, instead, mental health professionals decide to ground their treatments in objectivity and reunite the body and mind? Then we can work together to create a world where we can all thrive, not just survive.

CHAPTER 10

THE IMPORTANCE OF STEWARDSHIP IN BUSINESS

By **JASON SHUPP**

When I was 17, I graduated from high school and swore two things: I would not move back to St. Louis and I would never work in the family business.

I was always proud of the family business. It provided me with a wonderful childhood and hard-earned work ethic over four summers of high school. But beyond that, it was never a part of me and I wanted nothing more to do with it.

I did well with my commitment for 12 years. I lived in various places throughout the country for various lengths of time. I earned a BA in Biology and enjoyed an eclectic professional pathway which included being a whitewater and snowmobile guide, an EMT, a karate instructor, and an industrial rigger.

But shortly before my 30th birthday, I broke my commitment to myself and accepted my Dad's offer to come work for him. And upon my return to the business, my paradigm about legacy began to change. As I was learning the biz, I would hear more of our customers I was working with say things like "your grandfather put my grandpa's roof on and your Dad did my Dad's home...". Strangers would ask about how my family was doing and wish my parents well.

As I eventually transitioned to the president of the company, with ownership to follow, the weight of the business's success was now on my shoulders. The weight of the business's reputation and legacy was equally heavy.

See, my father was G2 (second generation). During his tenure, his brother-in-law ended up with ownership in the business as well. Ultimately, that partnership failed and the business stayed with my father. This failure came with great consequence to the relationships of our extended family, the mental and physical health of those intimately involved, and the company culture.

So when I joined the company, my brother and I were aware of the expectation to eventually share ownership and management. I already had a clear example of what happened when a family partnership failed. My brother and I were determined not to let that happen again.

Except it did. The crux of my family business journey was the three-year dissolution of my partnership with my brother and the family fallout that came after.

My brother and I invested much time, energy, and money surrounding ourselves with knowledge and resources. Our belief at the start of the journey was this would prevent history from repeating itself. After my brother's departure from the business, I realized all of my family business "training" was really meant to prepare me to survive *when* history repeated itself.

As my tenure with the business grew, so did my obligation to the staff's health, success, and solvency. I saw that the extended family of the business could not simply be a lower priority than the bloodline of my biological family. After the partnership legally ended, I spent the next year recovering from what I have dubbed Entrepreneurial Traumatic Stress Disorder (ETSD) ™. On the other side of that year, with the stress of uncertainty behind me, I was able to reflect on my experiences. I sought answers for what I needed to do to take care of myself. The answer was as much, if not more about taking care of others.

I kept coming back to the concept of stewardship — the responsible management of something entrusted to your care. I compartmentalized three facets of my life that involve stewardship.

My first lesson in stewardship:
During succession, focus on the chain rather than the link.

Each generation of management or ownership represents a link that is one part of a larger chain, the business. I found myself reeling over the ways the business transition could have been better. We tried to follow the playbook, as this process is well documented by a litany of experts. We still ended up fractured in the end, though.

I finally accepted the past, not just as something that I can't change, but rather as something that is understandably meant to be. The previous generation has its own narrative, bound by both opportunities and limitations. This is true of my tenure too.

To transcend those limitations, I learned that succession should not be hierarchical. Succession is a conversation, not a presentation.

Stewardship only works if the organization is the focus and not the steward. Here are a few questions I found value in considering around this idea:

- Do my personal goals conflict with the business needs?
- What is my current engagement with the company vision?
- Are there people who are better equipped to lead than the current or designated leaders?
- Does retirement need to be the main signal for transition?

The transition to the new steward must be collaborative. I am not my father. I grew up in a different generation and socioeconomic factors will influence me accordingly. Different technologies are available to me. Consequently, I am going to do things differently.

When I work with my future successor, I need to teach the values of the organization so they are understood and honored. I need to collaborate with my successor on the best methods to implement strategies and I need to be prepared to be uncomfortable. I need to listen to my successor to understand their personal narrative and what allows them success. Yes, there is much to consider on the business side such as shares, net worth, voting rights, taxes, benefits, payments, etc, but I can't lose sight of the mutual dynamic of the transition.

My second lesson in stewardship:
Financial security is for everyone—not just the leaders.

During my time with the business, I have become quite the student of estate planning. I have found myself standing on many a soapbox about the topic. I was set up for success as my parents did a good job of having structure in place. During the G2/G3 transition, I had to participate in the succession process for the sake of the business. Ultimately, it was very comforting having a plan for my life's affairs. As a father, I was early to apply best practices for my son so he was set up for success with any obstacles life may throw our way.

These experiences have helped me become more mindful of stewardship as it pertains to my staff. I realized I had looked at employer best practices as more of a snapshot. Essentially, I could bullet point the employee benefits on a piece of paper and use it during a review to highlight for purposes of retention. I could use the same bullet points for purposes of recruitment. It was really a list of what your life can look like by employment at this moment, usually expressed over a relatively small time period such as a year.

To be fair, this worked fairly well for a while. But the longer I stayed, the more I realized I could do to make sure my employees were getting the security and support they needed.

Every year I looked to improve company benefits, from increasing benefit days to disability insurance, shortening work hours to implementing tuition reimbursement. I would backfill positions to create space for professional advancement. I mentored people with the risk they would outgrow opportunities at the business. I have referred financial advisors and estate attorneys to various members of the team. I have participated in retirement exits and know it can be done with patience, grace, and respect.

One of my trusted financial advisors shared with me an ethos of his business. I modified the sentiment for my role and thought of it often at review time. "It is my job to fund the value of the role, not the lifestyle of the person". In many ways, sadly, this has to be true. The institutional constructs in (American) business force certain standards for businesses to stay profitable or be competitive. I believe consideration of our human resources in business can be more than a math equation.

Again, a business is really a group of people and the quality of those lives have to be considered. I want to find the opportunity to help the staff achieve financial security in their lifetime. This goes beyond just funding a 401K. It is about identifying barriers and helping those get over them. It is about providing structure, guidance, and opportunity to invest in their life. I have already begun to share this knowledge with my son. Generational knowledge is to be shared with the organization too. My goal is to strategically infuse this financial stewardship into the leadership, culture, and operations of the business.

My third lesson in stewardship:
When possible, connect philanthropy to business strategy and problem prevention.

Our company has always had a history of taking care of people. My grandfather was a generous man who took really good care of his roofers. My father was much the same, and with the scale of the business was able to do much more. Sponsorships, donations, staff bonuses, and a general giving attitude were his norms. Times, as they say, were changing when my brother and I took over in 2007. Through all of that, our culture of giving continued. In fact, the company's efforts over the next several years were to formalize the giving programs and work them into the strategic objectives of the business. This was met with varying levels of success as implementation is not always realized as well as intention.

In my journey with philanthropy, I have learned that giving is personal. For some, it includes loss or sacrifice. For others, it could be a calling. For me, it stems from a desire to do good through value-applied business practices. As I dove into this community, I asked myself many questions about whether the organizations we supported were making an impact and whether that impact was sustainable. As I considered these factors, I determined that strategic philanthropy can have the highest impact when it prevents problems from developing or worsening.

From there, I gravitated towards missions that focused on youth wellness, like Shape the Sky, Kidsmart, Living Well Foundation (Camp Jumpstart), and the National Interscholastic Cycling Association (NICA). Organizations like these share my belief that by getting involved early, they can help prevent problems in children's lives before they start or become too difficult to manage. As a parent and a legacy business owner, I appreciate that social problem solving is on a generational timeline. That is one of the facets of stewardship – the problems I work on today will likely be solved when I'm gone, trusting that today's efforts will lead to those solutions.

When my father made me the job offer in 2003, I asked him how long I needed to stay in order to be able to leave without repercussions if I decided the roofing industry was not for me. He told me three years. It took me four to fully decide to stay. Now, nearly two decades later, I am honored to be a part of something bigger than myself, something that has impacted so many others, something that has connected me to a larger community, and something that can live beyond me. This is the true meaning of stewardship, and I'm so grateful to have learned it from my family business.

CHAPTER 11

7 LESSONS FROM THE RACE TO CURE CANCER

By JEFF NORSKOG

Dr. Paul Janssen (lovingly referred to by colleagues and friends as "Dr. Paul"), was a legend of the pharmaceutical industry. A Belgian doctor who founded Janssen Pharmaceutica in 1953 and later sold the company to multinational giant Johnson & Johnson (J&J), he was a pioneer in introducing systems thinking and immunotherapy into treating chronic diseases, including cancer. He was also the first Western drugmaker to enter the China market after the Cultural Revolution, where he significantly evolved his thinking about medicine after coming to understand the central role – developed over millennia in the Middle Kingdom – of natural plant extracts in preventing and treating illness.

One important disciple of Dr. Paul's was my father, Jerry, a Montana native and J&J executive whose wanderlust found him in China in 1990, chosen by Dr. Paul to implement his vision for Xian Janssen. Xian Janssen was one of the first and most successful pharmaceutical joint ventures ever established in China.

There Remains Much to be Done

One of Dr. Paul's favorite sayings was "there remains much to be done". He knew first hand the complexity of chronic, heterogeneous disease. So when my dad retired from J&J in his early 50s, he knew that there was still unfinished business for him to carry out that would honor Dr. Paul's legacy.

Upon returning to North America, Jerry networked himself into a group of like-minded scientists, entrepreneurs, doctors and investors led by Silicon Valley technology innovator James Dao, his brother Tom and a stellar team of scientists. They founded Genyous Biomed. Years later in 2016, then-Vice President Joe Biden would launch the National Cancer Moonshot, with a goal to compress 10 years of advancement in cancer prevention and treatment into 5 years, and to find vaccine-based immunotherapy options.

But the Genyous team and its first commercial spinoff Omnitura Therapeutics was well ahead of the curve. In 2002, they were already asking themselves: What if the launch pad, the rocket, the fuel and all of the private sector contractors that fed into the Moonshot were fundamentally flawed? To use the famous line from Hollywood's *Apollo 13*, what if we had to shut down "the whole smash" and start all over again?

Jerry and his partners in Omnitura understood how and why the pharmaceutical industry had become reliant on "blockbuster" cancer drugs that targeted a single disease pathway. In the early years, these treatments were cause for hope. Occasionally, a patient's gene-expression profile might reveal a perfect match for a compound that could target it, shutting down its expression and reversing disease. While many important advances have been made in specific diseases, benefits for the majority of more common adult cancers have been minimal. Drugs cost hundreds of millions of dollars to develop, and those costs are passed on to patients, often while only adding a few months to life and causing distressing side effects, all diminishing a patient's quality of life.

Dream Big and Other Big Thinkers Will Follow

Genyous, which by then had recruited partners from leading cancer research universities – including BC Cancer Research Centre in Canada, Harvard Medical, Johns Hopkins, UCSD, UCLA and Stanford in the United States and York in the UK – knew that a paradigm shift was needed.

We live in a big world with big challenges that need big solutions. Once you establish a goal to meet those challenges, like minds magnetize around those goals and that's when things get really interesting, and achievable. Teamwork is a beautiful thing.

James Dao was a powerful force, intent on better scientific discovery. He found people who shared his frustration and vision, who were looking past single target drugs with a whole systems biology approach. They were looking into plants. They were working to shift the paradigm, every day, in the lab, and they were getting excited by what they found.

The group distilled their big dreams into the following philosophy: to accelerate the cure, control and quality of life for people living with cancer through integration, collaboration and application of evidence-based knowledge derived from natural, pharmaceutical, and biomedical science and practice.

Always Go Back to the Drawing Board

Drawing bigger circles around bigger problems was the team's initial approach. They went back through history. They looked at everything. They took concepts apart and put them back together in new ways. They brought thought leaders together and brainstormed with hundreds of global experts.

The group started with what they knew: most researchers deploy single molecule drugs when fighting cancer. But the human body is complex. Disease is complex. Cancer is complex. A great asset is our immune system, which is designed and evolutionarily conserved as the line of defense against internal and external threats. First up was to better understand how to empower the immune system to do the job it was designed to do: recognize disease and modulate the systems back to normal.

The roadmap to their goals was supported by a few key elements:

- Engaging across disciplines of practice and healing philosophies (traditional, natural and biomedical)
- Inclusivity, collaboration and leadership to achieve patient-relevant outcomes – cure, care, control and quality of life
- Tolerance of risk, failure, dismissal, and rejection as integral parts of the pursuit of innovation to accelerate substantial advance in the control of cancer

As they worked through their research on cancer, they discovered that formulating various specific plants together created a new synergy that promised to combat cancer by modulating - and potentially even rebooting- the immune system.

This was game-changing for our project and a potential paradigm shift for the industry, and even for human civilization.

New Approaches Need New Metrics

The ultimate goal is to empower the immune system to return the whole biological system to a state of cancer control and wellness. That metric will speak for itself: one loved-one saved. One less loved-one to mourn. The numbers are staggering. When the numbers come down, we all win.

However, it will take some time for us to get there. Our drug must be shown through rigorous clinical trial to be effective, safe, and an advance on existing therapies. This is the basis for Food and Drug Administration (FDA) regulatory approval. Until then, to build confidence with pharmaceutical investors, we need to show success metrics that map back to theirs, metrics that they understand. We have many to show but we don't have all, because we have a different approach - a new approach. And our new approach requires different metrics.

Omnitura has raised $18 Million from a community of private investors who not only understand this but, in fact, embrace it. They have been willing to take on greater risk for greater reward, because they know that the existing approach isn't serving enough patients sufficiently, and they insist on more innovative and impactful solutions. These are true "angel" investors who have watched over our project with love and support.

We have come a long way. Our journey has celebrated many wins. We successfully completed Phase I clinical trials proving safety with observations of efficacy. Yet in front of us we still have the heavy lifting of funding our Phase II trial. Funding a new paradigm? Risky. More times than we can count, we have been told "Wow. This is exciting. Come back when you have finished Phase II."

While our science gets people really excited, many pharmaceutical industry investors can't, or or are unwilling to, wrap their heads around our new approach and are skeptical of our plant-based solutions. They are busy with the development of an ever-expanding pipeline of single target drugs.

We have come to learn this: our approach doesn't map to our investors' or industry's understanding of drugs because they are largely invested in the current paradigm - single-function, single target. Our approach - multi-functional and multi-targeted therapeutics - requires a new mindset and metrics adapted to a new paradigm.

Undertaking pilot studies, developing appropriate measures to document mechanism of action, and doing proof-of-principle trials to prove our hypothesis takes time and money. It takes a while for people to get their heads around new ideas, but advancing medicine that saves lives can't afford to stall out.

Create Your Own Timing and Momentum

Recognizing the potential of plants to be developed as prescription drugs, the FDA introduced FDA Botanical Drug Guidelines in 2004. We are among the very first to go down this path but we are early; there is little to no funding. Investors want to see a clearly defined mode of action while FDA has no requirements other than demonstrating efficacy and safety. Again, new approaches need new metrics. But it's coming.

We've moved forward with our drug development digging into all of the regulations required to receive FDA approval. The process is almost overwhelming for a startup group. We like to call receiving FDA approval the Mount Everest of this process.

Because of the steep climb involved in dealing with the FDA, it would be easy to sit back and say our timing is bad. In fact, ours is an ever changing landscape, full of challenges, mostly headwinds, only occasional tail winds. Our timing was good with earlier trials; we achieved success with Phase I, but the push into Phase II, requires substantial sums of capital.

However, we never want to allow outside forces to control our timing.

Instead, one of our core beliefs is that we strive every day to create our own momentum.

And we stay on it, everyday, researching, testing, trials and more. And while we raise the funding for our own trial, we'll put our science to work in partner trials. The everyday goal is to prove our science and create pathways to market, to get this product to people, as many people as possible, as soon as possible.

This has led us to look into creating a version of our drug aimed at prevention which would allow us to move forward without FDA approval. This would feel really good, as it would jump start our prevention drug platform, one of Genyous' original company mandates. We want to put our science to use - "translational research" - to support the continuum of health from wellness to disease, survival and death.

The idea is to stay well. We believe a bio-pharmaceutical grade, science-based supplement can support this. Yes, our focus has been on immuno-oncology drugs for late stage disease and cancer but we will put our learnings to use to help people in every way that we can. So, while we wait for FDA approval of our clinical therapeutic, we will keep the momentum going by launching a nutraceutical called Thriva™.

Celebrate the Wins

Some people are so focused on the big win that they forget to enjoy the process along the way. Living a good mission everyday is a win.

One of the best ways to maintain momentum and motivation for your project is to celebrate every small win that comes along. Also examining small wins assures that you won't miss something. A small win can sometimes be a catalyst for a necessary pivot.

Achieving goals and successfully navigating obstacles is always worth celebrating.

Clear a Path For The Next Generation

We have big dreams and big plans for this project but we also have a realistic outlook. We understand that we may not be the ones who carry this project over the finish line and that's okay.

This project has been a higher calling for everyone involved. Whether our project delivers the end goal whilst in our hands, or brings success for others in the future, everyone involved feels great about their contribution.

CHAPTER 12

THE PURPOSE OF PAIN

By **JEREMY HUNT**

Is there an obstacle in front of you right now? A pain point in your life at this present moment?

There is no solution in talking about it or by wishing it will go away or trying to find ways around it. The only way is forward and through.

Accepting and learning from pain is an opportunity to find the solution, purpose, and become a more effective leader. It is not merely experiencing the emotion caused by the source of the pain, it is about going through it, coming out on the other side a better person. By going through you become an example, have a story to tell, and ultimately can influence others in a positively powerful way. Oftentimes, the way through the pain leads us to the solution and our purpose in life. It was through the pain that I found my healing and purpose.

After graduating college in 1999 I had one great opportunity after the next. I was a full-time youth director by 22 years of age, business owner by 28, and by the time I was an associate pastor at a megachurch at 38 years old, I thought I had really gone to the next level and I planned to keep climbing. That did not happen! — I quickly fell off that mountain, and hard!

After less than one year as a pastor at one of America's fastest-growing churches, I voluntarily resigned in December of 2014. During that brief opportunity my family and I made a positive impact in many lives, but I still failed. I didn't fail because of a clash of culture or character, but one of capacity. I did not have the leadership skills to lead at that level. I had hit what John Maxwell calls my "lid," the cap of leadership that prevents effectiveness from increasing beyond a certain point.

I recognized that my lid was impacting my team and the ability to lead effectively, so I stepped down. It was devastating. I shattered inside. All the effort, sacrifice, and hope to pursue "my calling" fell apart.

I wish I could say that I picked up the pieces from this experience and led my family effectively in the years that followed, but I did not. While trying to come to terms with my failure, I decided to move the family back to Minnesota and I returned to the business I helped start a few years earlier, but by the middle of 2016 my role in the business and the partnership ended. The following year I had to file bankruptcy.

If I fell off the mountain in 2014, I would have fallen into the abyss in 2020 when my marriage of over 22 years was coming to an end. I was drinking heavily to wash down the pain, retreating from social activities, depressed, and would pace back and forth in the middle of the night. Rock bottom of the abyss came in November of 2020 when I went out for dinner with some friends and fell apart emotionally. At that moment, it was evident I needed help and the following day I stumbled across a Facebook advertisement for a coaching & mentoring program.

By December of 2020, I was fully immersed in a journey of personal transformation, healing, and pursuit of my life purpose that continues to this day. In less than a year every aspect of my life has been changed for the better. Most importantly, I was able to let go of negative emotions and experience peace and joy. I can be grateful and honor my past, and even be thankful for the failures and pain because it created an opportunity for change.

After spending much of the last 7 years without it, I was able to realign my purpose in life and I'm on a mission again. My voice is my mission. A mission to tell others that we all can move from pain to purpose. While my journey involved dozens of lessons, in this chapter I'd like to talk about "acceptance" and "going through" to find your purpose and mission.

Leaders Accept Pain

Acceptance is the first and most important step because it is the doorway to move from pain to purpose. When we accept what is, we go from focusing on the pain to possibilities. When we walk through the doorway of acceptance it is now possible to let go of the negative emotions.

It can be helpful to look at this like a flow of energy. There is an energy behind all types of pain such as stress, anxiety, anger, rejection, resentment and so much more. It is a natural reaction to be against the pain in our lives. But when we are against something it creates resistance and that tension creates negative emotions.

When we accept what is, it creates peace because both positive and negative cannot exist within us at the same moment. Acceptance is about letting go, not holding on. We are letting go of what we can not control and the solutions exist in what we can control. We've all heard the quote that "you can't change the world, you can only change yourself." A weight lifted from me when I learned that I did not need to resist the negative, but could accept it instead.

Accepting pain doesn't mean that you become passive and do nothing. Like Eckhart Tolle says, "Accept - then act." I began to understand that my peace and joy were not dependent on anybody or anything around me. I was now prepared to take action by focusing on what I can control, which started with my mindset and motivations.

To change the way we feel, we must change the way we think. This begins by telling ourselves the truth. When we think negative thoughts about ourselves, we are not telling the truth. If we talked to others this way, we would not have any friends.

After years of disappointment, failure, and rejection I started to believe that I was not good enough, was not a "real man," and I started believing many other lies about myself. In my work on myself, I learned that I need to start telling myself the truth. There are many ways to say this, but I think of words like retrain, rewire, and renew. One way to do this is by repeating what Larry Bilotta calls "tiny stories." Here's how I practice doing this:

Step 1: Three Words

Identify 3 words that describe you at your best. You can do this by coming up with 3 memories: when you were your authentic self, by expressing yourself and how you feel as who you truly are as a person. While this is the best way to do it, you can also come up with 3 words that illustrate who you would like to become. When I did this, I chose Fun, Confident, and Inspirational.

Choosing the word "Fun" was important because I allowed myself to lose the authentic "fun" part of myself and believed the lie that I was no longer a "fun" person because of how I was feeling.

Have fun with this because you will manifest these words in your life and they will become your reality.

Step 2: Place & Time

After choosing your 3 words, think back to a specific place and time when you were expressing yourself in accord with each word. For example, when I chose the word "Fun", I came up with a memory of laughing, talking, and being my authentic silly self at my friend Marci's home in the year 2000.

Word: Fun
Place: Marci's Home, Time: January 2000.

Step 3: Tiny Story

Come up with a brief statement or story that tells you how you express (or will express) each word. For example:

Word: Fun
Place: Marci's Home, Time: January 2000.
Tiny Story: I'm a fun person who loves to joke, laugh, and be silly with people so they have fun as well.

Other examples:

- Grateful - I'm grateful for everything. I am grateful for the pain because it makes me grow
- Love - I love myself and everybody around me loves me
- Calm - I am calm, safe, and secure, and I make others feel this way

Over the next 30 days tell yourself these "tiny stories" as often as possible, multiple times a day. When you are going through pain, the pain itself can be a natural "alarm clock" to tell yourself these stories. When you feel the pain, don't dwell on it. Instead, tell yourself a "tiny story" as often as the pain surfaces.

Turn that pain into purpose by telling yourself the truth. The most important thing is that you believe in yourself and who you are, that is where the change happens. However, there is a very real impact on how others look at you and start treating you. There are many ways to describe it, some call it "mirroring", the "law of attraction", and so on.

When I started applying my 3 words it changed how I felt and I started to become Fun, Confident, and Inspirational once again. I walked through the doorway of acceptance and this was just the beginning of the change in my internal and external environment.

Leaders Go Through Pain

Going Through is not allowing the pain to control you or impact you in any negative way. It is not passive. It is about taking wise action! It is also hard work, no passivity here! When some people started to see the changes in me, they said, "Oh, it's just easy for you." Hell no! It wasn't easy! It's never easy. It takes a lot of courage to face our fears.

Every day in my delivery business there are obstacles in our way such as accidents, construction, etc., and we have to reroute ourselves but we don't lose sight of the delivery destination. "Going Through" can be a rerouting but never about going backward or giving up.

In Ryan Holiday's book *The Obstacle Is the Way,* he writes "there is always a way out or another route to get to where you need to go, so that setbacks or problems are always expected and never permanent, making certain that what impedes us can empower us."

By choosing to go through we are focusing on the present moment and all the possibilities that exist. The energy required to talk about the past needs to be used in a more positive and creative way of thinking to discover solutions.

"Going Through" forces us to ask questions and get the answers. When we do this we move from focusing on the pain/obstacle to purpose/solution. This past Summer in July of 2021, I had a huge obstacle in front of me with my delivery business. There was an accidental billing error with one of our largest national accounts. The result required that all three businesses that partner together on this project come up with tens of thousands of dollars in less than two months. With credit lines unavailable and cash flow already designated to other areas, this was a huge problem.

Looking back, I feel fortunate to have already had months of training in personal transformation when this obstacle presented itself to me. I made the choice that the only pathway was through. I didn't know what the solution was going to be, but even when I put my head on the pillow each night I very consciously told myself I was NOT going to lose sleep about this.

I also chose not to talk about the issue with other people unless it was about discussing possibilities. I chose to practice being present and living in the "power of the now." This allowed me to experience peace, believing that we would come up with a solution that would ensure that our drivers would be paid on time.

And it worked. Not one of the business partners pointed fingers at each other, each had the mindset that we were going to work together and with our customer to find a solution. In the end, it required personal sacrifice from each of us, extra work, leaning on the trust already established between us and our customer, but we got through it with a stronger bond established between all involved.

After months of making the hard but wise choice to go through, I developed my own creed that I began to live by. It has become a consistent reminder of all that I have learned and has helped me be present each day, especially when seeing the next obstacle/opportunity in front of me.

My Creed of Presence

I will be present today
I know that all paths involve pain,
I choose not to look for a way around
I go through

I will experience peace and joy
I will be the best version of myself today
No matter what my life situation
I accept things as they are

I am grateful
I am grateful for these obstacles
Because they are opportunities

No matter what comes my way
I am not dependent on the external
I accept peace and joy

I will forgive, to be forgiven
I will walk in integrity, and I will shine
When I feel the pain
I go through

No matter what I feel
No matter what is in my way
I will see the possibilities
I go through

I have good and healthy relationships
God, I give you my heart today
I give you my relationships
May Your will be done
Make me a vessel for your will

I will be present now
When the obstacles come
I will know what to do
What not to do
I am experiencing freedom, peace, and joy!

You may find it valuable to come up with a creed like this for yourself to help you accept and go through the pain in your life. Either way, remember that accepting and going through your pain is the true path to leadershipl — first leading yourself, and then leading those around you.

CHAPTER 13

THE VALUE OF COACHING

By JESSIE WILLIAMS

Here's a confession: I used to *hate* work-related coaching and training. As a former 9-to-5 employee, I remember being dragged away from my billable hours to hear speakers try to teach us about leadership skills and personal development. I thought it was nonsense that had nothing to do with the numbers on the sheets I was in charge of. But once I started out by myself and owned my own business, my whole outlook changed.

There's an enormous difference between being an employee and a business owner. As an employee, I just had to be physically present for a certain amount of time. Oftentimes, employees can slack off for half of their workday and still get enough done to satisfy their bosses. The buck didn't stop with us, and we were only a small piece of the pie but as a business owner, I *am* the pie.

When starting a business, your physical and mental health has to be in top shape. Everything is a balance. You can't take many sick days if you expect your company to grow. You can't show up with a bad attitude or even just feeling sluggish after an afternoon lunch. You quite literally cannot afford it. Don't get me wrong, you don't have to work around the clock like everyone seems to think. But you do have to constantly be present, ready to perform and nurture relationships with clients.

Now, I fully appreciate all of the lessons I used to think were just guru mumbo jumbo. Some things are as small as learning the right way to get out of bed in the morning. With a regular job, I used to just walk out the door without giving much thought to my morning routine or the mindset it was putting me in. But these days, I pay attention to the small details. I start my days with gratitude exercises, eat breakfast, work out, and finally catch up on emails before I look at any other work items. With this routine, I'm ready to perform at a high level until 7 p.m., rather than checking out for half the workday and going home at 5 p.m.

If you want to make it anywhere in life, you have to have some help in developing yourself. That goes not only for your career and your business, but also for yourself as a person. Where should you turn to when you're trying to improve yourself or just learn something new? Many people look to books, YouTube videos, or other depersonalized instruction. But I am a firm believer in the power of coaching – that the best way to make progress is with a real mentor who can guide and motivate you every step of the way.

In this chapter, I will lay out the four coaches who have had the biggest positive impact on my life and business career. Each is indispensable to my success and proves why good coaching is so worth the investment.

Fitness coach:

Let's face it – America has a fitness problem. As one of the most obese nations on the planet, we're clearly not doing a great job when it comes to exercising on our own. That's where a fitness coach comes in. When you have a specific goal you want to achieve, whether it be weight loss or a personal record, you want someone to help you get there. With a coach, you get that feeling that someone else is going to be there with you to help motivate you to get out of bed early.

The greatest benefit I get from fitness coaching is morning training sessions. It's not a coincidence that so many successful people work out first thing in the morning. As an entrepreneur, the hormones produced from working up a good sweat give you a rush that boosts your mood and energy for the entire day. It can make a big difference when serving customers or connecting with potential clients.

After a successful workout session, you feel like you can do anything you put your mind to. I am currently able to flip a 400-pound tire, something I never dreamed I would be able to do when I first started with my coach. The mindset he's instilled in me is that we can do anything we tell our bodies to do. It may hurt for a few minutes, but once you're through the short period of pain, you're so much stronger. We can apply that tool – productive suffering – to our lives and business careers too. That's why I'm always telling my fitness coach to give me exercises I hate doing. Currently, my punisher is running. I've always hated it – I never saw the point – but knowing now from my trainer that it's so good for the body, I've set a goal to easily run five miles next year.

Health and Wellness coach:

The importance of health for entrepreneurs goes beyond just keeping good care of your physical well-being. Arguably more consequential is your mental state – and not just mental health in the way we traditionally think of it, but the little things we can do to make our brains more productive throughout the entire day. I've seen major improvements in this area of my life since I started working with a health and wellness coach.

You might wonder what the difference is between this person and a therapist. It's all about the degree of help you need. A therapist assesses, diagnoses, and treats, while my health and wellness coach works with me to maintain healthy habits to ensure I maintain a healthy balance between my personal and professional life. She's who I'll call for advice if I have a horrible day at work or need techniques to boost my productivity.

One practice I've learned is focused breathing when I'm tasked with tough situations. I've always hated the idea of meditating, probably because I'd never tried it before, but when I'm about to "fly off the handle" because of something stressful at work, breathing truly helps.

My mental health coach has not only helped me stay calm in high-pressure environments; she's also guided me to become a happier person overall. For example, she's taught me that if someone is being unnecessarily mean in a business interaction, the chances are that they are just having a bad day. I've had to learn how to not take that negative feedback personally, because I used to waste so much energy being upset and annoyed.

As a business owner, I simply don't have the time to deal with those emotions — they are unproductive when on the other hand, you could just externalize those feelings and deal with the situation when you've cooled off. There's nothing wrong with taking time to clear your mind, even if a task or correspondence has to wait until the next day.

Business coach:

Accountants have tons of skills that help with so many aspects of a new business. We can crunch numbers, stay organized, and make sure the books are balanced. But there's one crucial piece of entrepreneurship for which my background in tax and accounting left me woefully unprepared: sales. An accountant at a large firm could go years on end without ever speaking with an established client, let alone a potential one. Faced with the task of growing a new business, acquiring new business and selling to new customers quickly became my biggest task. I sought out the help of my first business coach to make sure it wasn't also my greatest liability.

Starting out with zero clients, our first task was to fill a pipeline with prospective clients. We knew we'd start getting more and more business through referrals once we did good work with the first few clients, but clinching those was the toughest part of the process. Although I enjoyed speaking, my coach helped me polish up my skills on how to talk to clients, how to best schedule meetings, and everything in between to make things easy and efficient. Aside from the nitty-gritty sales work, he pushed me to think about where I wanted my business to be in five and ten years.

My business coach stuck with us as we grew into a profitable business, giving us all the necessary tools to be successful. I can't imagine where I'd be today without him — certainly not in the position I'm in now. But as we approached a substantial number of sales and clients, we realized we needed a more detailed roadmap to grow further.

Growth coach:

Next, I looked for a coach who could give more specific and strategic advice for our growing business. I was at the point where instead of being desperate for clients, I could turn away those that weren't a good fit. Once the firm hit $250,000 in net revenue, I was hungry to hit half a million. To do that, I know we would have to somehow scale up, or possibly acquire and target more clients that fit our model. Either way, my business-growth coach has taught me that the key to growth is still, in fact, sales.

He had a lot of suggestions. He suggested I block out 90 minutes a day for structured sales activities, one of my favorites, and showed me new habits in scheduling and color-coding to improve my productivity during that time. I'm always looking to fill up my client pipeline – if someone leaves, I need to have one or more replacements lined up. My growth coach reminds me to ask myself questions like, "Who do I need to follow up on?" "Who do I need to sign agreements with?" and "Who do I need to book a call with who said they were interested in our services?" With his coaching, we're well on our way to hitting our revenue goal.

Why coaching?

Why not just try to learn everything yourself? It's cheaper and a smaller investment than hiring a coach, some might say. For me, that investment – financial and otherwise – you put into coaching is actually one of the main reasons it works so well. Let's just take the gym as an example. If you're paying $10 or $15 per month for a gym membership, what is going to be your incentive for getting up and making it there every morning? Each time you hit the snooze button, you're only losing a couple of dimes. If you're paying for sessions with a personal trainer, on the other hand, you're going to show up or otherwise be wasting money you can't afford to let go down the drain. Committing to a paid coach gives you more financial incentive to put in the work and improve yourself when you're feeling unmotivated.

Coaching also gets you where you want to go quicker. Let's say I want to learn how to climb a rope. Without a coach, I have to read up on the technique, watch videos, and then finally go to the gym. Once I get there, I have to worry about possibly injuring myself because there isn't an expert there watching me to ensure my form is correct. Without instant feedback from an instructor, I'll have to video record myself on the rope and watch it later, doubling the time it takes to learn. The same concept applies to business coaching. You could certainly read a business book or take a self-taught course, but neither of those is going to get you where you want to be as quick as a real coach will.

Finally, coaching allows you to know you're doing things the right way with a level of detail that self-instruction cannot provide. For example, my husband, an amateur weightlifter, is much more frugal than I am – he's gotten very physically fit without ever spending a dime on a trainer or a coach. The other day he was trying to learn how to deadlift. Unlike a lot of the other exercises he performs, this one comes with a high chance of injury if not executed correctly. So while going through his normal routine of watching YouTube instructional videos, he started worrying that he could seriously hurt his back if he didn't do everything right. For the first time, he asked me to arrange a session with my fitness trainer. The level of detail and individualized feedback he felt he needed for a deadlift was just too high to go into the exercise without one.

Coaching has had such a huge impact on me that I will soon be passing along my knowledge and experience with my own coaching program. I hope to deliver what past coaches have delivered for me: accountability that motivates, detail that clarifies, and efficiency that quickens. And whether you work with me or a coach of your choosing, I hope you will take the chance to find out how much greater your life can be when you invest in the right coaches. I promise you, it will be even better than you can imagine.

CHAPTER 14

FUTURE-FOCUSED ACCOUNTING: YOUR PROFITABILITY GAMECHANGER

By **JIM DOWNES**

Most business leaders don't actually know their businesses. Wait...*most business leaders don't actually know their businesses?!*

While this statement may seem shocking, it's the harsh reality of firms large and small around the globe.

Sure, most leaders can whip off their mission statements and share the products and services they've brought to market. They can give the impression that they are innovative thinkers with their fingers on the pulse of their brand, the market, and the world at large. They can take large-scale actions, thinking they are moving their businesses forward.

And still, they can be shooting in the dark.

While these leaders may excel at what they know, they all have one blind spot in common – and it's a big one. They don't know their numbers, let alone understand them.

And if you don't know your numbers, how can you truly know where your brand stands, and where your brand is going?

Accounting Can Be An Asset

Most companies are reactionary when it comes to accounting and finance – and many don't even realize it!

As a business leader, you may feel you have all your ducks in a row when it comes to the story you are telling about last year's financials. Maybe you feel ready to go when tax season rolls around. You may even have some good talking points about the ups and downs of the past year, and an overall summary that you can recite in your sleep. Now, don't get me wrong, this information is crucial to have on hand! However, it is only the tip of the iceberg.

There is a lost opportunity emanating from most accounting departments worldwide. Operating merely as company historians, most are past-focused, missing out on all of the opportunities that exist in the present and future.

Your accounting shouldn't just recap last year's numbers – that's simply reporting. And while most accounting and finance professionals typically claim to analyze business performance, they often stop at reporting the prior period's performance, rather than continuing onto the strategic stage that is necessary for success.

Most companies view their accounting departments as cost centers rather than revenue generators. But what if your accounting could be your company's strategic weapon, propelling you towards increased productivity and profitability?

If your firm is ready to combat stagnancy and experience lasting growth, it's time to embody a data-driven, future-focused approach to your financial statements.

A true game-changer for entrepreneurs and multinational corporations alike, future-focused accounting does more than just recap historical information. Rather, it utilizes the past to understand the present and propel the future.

Making the Shift

My first experience in the world of future-focused accounting met me face-to-face back when I was a CPA, when a then-client approached me, asking for my advice as their financial advisor. *Jim, what do you think we should do differently in the future?*

Though seemingly simple, this question stopped me in my tracks. I had completed the company's year-end reports. I knew everything about how their business had performed in the previous calendar year overall. But despite having my head buried in their financial statements and reports, I realized how limited my perspective truly was.

Looking back, my reporting was on point – but my accounting was not. I had little to no strategic input to provide my client with about which products were profitable and which were draining their cash flow. To that same end, I hadn't looked to the future in regards to the cost-efficiency of their sales and marketing efforts. All in all, I had no concrete view of what was going on in my client's business in the present – not to mention any strategic guidance for increasing profitability for the future.

It shouldn't take being a deer in the headlights to understand the importance of strategic thinking when it comes to your company's financials. However, it is all too common a situation for business leaders and accounting professionals alike to be met with – usually in the face of a rejected loan, an unforeseen cash-flow problem, or even a global crisis.

It's time to change that, and be strategic, not just reactionary. It's time to keep the past, present, *and* future top of mind.

Accounting for the Past

Effective accounting means not just reporting the past, but actually accounting for it. *Accounting* and *accountability* come from the same root word, after all. But traditionally, accounting deliverables are focused on what has occurred in the past and lax on addressing what future changes need to happen.

We have all heard the words *you need to measure it to manage it,* but if your measures are incorrect, inconsistent, or delayed, you are at a strategic dead-end. Weak management leads to weak accountability which leads to poor financial performance, and if you view the numbers side of your business as just that – a bunch of numbers – how can you ever get a true sense of where your firm is *truly* at?

It's time to take accountability for your business – starting with your accounting. After all, *accountability* isn't just about acknowledging the past but taking corrective actions to ensure future change.

While knowing how your company performed in the past is necessary, stopping there will keep you stagnant. True performance analysis – true accounting – means taking the data and not only knowing your numbers but *understanding* them.

When you know something without truly understanding it, it goes in one ear and out the other. This is what typically happens when business owners look at their financial statements. Sure, they might know some basic details – like how much cash is in the bank or their revenues or profit margins – but that is the extent of the matter.

Just as *acknowledgment* is not the same thing as *accountability*, *reporting* is not synonymous with *accounting*. True accounting highlights growth potentials and strategic improvements to propel you forward, not just recapping the actions of the past. True accounting understands the implications of what the data says and advises you to act accordingly.

Understanding the Present

Future-based accounting starts where historical accounting leaves off – right here and now, in the present. After all, if you were to truly *understand* your numbers, you would have a newfound ability to feel the pulse of your business at any moment in time – including this one.

I was once on a board of directors of a sizable company with a number of other directors, many of whom had accounting backgrounds. Our entire time in board meetings was spent analyzing the historical financial statements and asking questions about expense variances from the budget. Never in our meeting did we talk about the future, emerging industry trends, or what we could do to take advantage of new opportunities. We merely focused on figuring out the past due to questionable metrics, so there was no space or energy left to explore growth potentials.

With a more strategic approach, the team could have taken an accurate and action-oriented snapshot of the brand. We would have had a better ability to proactively overcome blind spots and take new action steps to move towards emerging opportunities.

Mapping for the Future

Sure, "getting by" in the present with some understanding of the past is a start — but it isn't much more than that. Treading the waters of today's reality and following the impulse of "shiny object syndrome" is *definitely* not the powerful form of leadership to aim for. To truly take your accounting to the next level, you must connect your company's current financial reality to your long-term business strategy, not just survive the situation that exists today.

To grow (or even survive) as a business in our ever-changing marketplace and world, you need to match your level of financial analysis with an equally effective vision. If you want to achieve new heights, you must rise by developing a compelling strategy for the months, years, and decades to come. How? By seeing past (and present) numbers not as "dated" but as "data," as metrics that can be utilized to inform and empower your next steps.

There is no better depiction of the importance of future-focused decision-making than the major disruption that COVID-19 has caused across countless industries. This past year has forced companies to adapt like never before. While many succeeded, others failed to pivot and went out of business as a result. Whether your journey was one of success or failure, we've all learned to never assume that "business as usual" will be the way forward.

With that powerful truth in mind, adapting to the future is something that all industries and brands – including yours – need to prioritize. After all, understanding how to increase your profitability, even as the world transforms, is key to your success and longevity.

When you have the full picture of what your finances look like – and what those numbers mean – you will be equipped to understand the scope of unforeseen opportunities and threats, and act strategically if and when they happen. In fact, when push comes to shove, future-focused thinking can save your business's life from a strategic standpoint, allowing you to be responsive rather than just reactionary.

Accountable Accounting in Action

Theory is one thing, but witnessing the concepts of strategic, future-focused accounting being put to practice is even more impactful, as the power of looking to tomorrow is undoubtedly an eye-opener for companies of all sizes and across all industries. Here are a few examples we have seen here at Blueprint CFO.

Consumer Products, Company Profitability

A consumer products company was struggling to wrap their head around their sales velocity by SKU, or the number of units they could sell when they were fully stocked with inventory. It's no wonder they were lost when it came to this – they were buying 2021 inventory based on 2017 sales! While they were somehow making it by, they were clearly looking to the past for guidance rather than the future. As such, they weren't fully taking advantage of product trends, nor were they being effective with their purchase planning.

Once the company began embodying strategic accounting practices, they realized that – based on current sales trends – they could re-price their products and increase their profit margins as a result. We improved their inventory accounting, allowing them a clearer view of their situation, along with the realization that they could increase prices without losing customer design.

Freight for the Future

A freight and logistics client was in complete financial disarray when they called upon our accounting futurists to step in and help them get organized. They had $7 million in accounts receivable, with no idea of who owed them what – the payments weren't being credited correctly…if at all!

When we stepped in, we came equipped with a concrete plan to help them get back on track and move towards the future. The results were truly astronomical, with $2 million in cash recovered by focusing on collection efforts, reducing the outstanding accounts receivable to $5 million.

SaaS Strategy

A software as a service client created a budget for the next year using how they performed the prior year as their basis. The budget came out with a $1 million profit for the year.

After guiding them through our strategic planning process, the budget stood at $1.5 million. Fast forward to the end of the year, and they not only met their goal but exceeded it at $1.7 million, another testament to the power of allotting regular time to understand how financials can be used to propel company profitability.

***

Do you know your business – I mean *really* know your business?

If you want the answer to be a resounding yes, it's time to stop putting out fires and getting caught in financial catch-22s. It's time to appreciate your numbers for the valuable assets they are, rather than seeing them as just another hoop to jump through to make ends meet.

All in all, it's time to stop letting reactionary thinking run your business, and craft a roadmap to profitability and longevity.

CHAPTER 15

DON'T DO IT ALL BY YOURSELF

By **JOSEPH CATANIA**

At the front of every successful business is a successful leader. But that leader certainly doesn't get to where they are on their own.

You can take your organization to a certain level with your brilliance, but it's only your team that can make you a leader and a winner. I've learned from several leadership positions over the years in management and marketing, but also as a stockbroker and in stock brokerage management, that you can't do it all yourself. It's about setting up your team to coincide with having goals, creating a business plan, having benchmarks, and so on.

Brilliant leaders cannot make a team succeed, but a group of committed and capable people with a purpose that's higher than personal glory, and with a humble leader, can make a winning team. It is impossible to do it by yourself, you need a great team to support you.

The realization that a team is integral to success is something I learned when I first started my career in the stock brokerage business, back in the 1980s and 1990s. I started off with just a phone book and a phone and was told to essentially just dial for dollars. I was working nights and weekends, and in doing so, built my business in about three years. And with that business, I had to be a jack of all trades. I had to worry about bookkeeping, hiring, firing, really anything that was part of owning your own business.

From there, I got into sales management and learned how to manage people, motivate people, hire people, fire people, and train people. Fast forward 15 years or so, and I was hired as the CFO of a law firm as well as its marketing director. This was a small firm with just three attorneys, but they were looking to grow and brought me on to help with this. They hired me to create a 10-year plan that would take them to be an eight-figure business.

It was at this point that I realized I needed some key things to successfully create this plan and do my job. I discovered that I couldn't do this work myself and I needed three important people with experience, loyalty, and a really good work ethic.

First, I needed a senior paralegal with 15-20 years of experience that would hire the other paralegals to assist the attorneys as well as fire people if necessary, while also doing the actual paralegal work. I also needed someone who could supervise the intake department because of all the calls that were coming into this personal injury law firm. I needed someone who could take a call, be empathetic, and explain why this law firm was the best to help with their needs. And lastly, I needed a good bookkeeper with a good background to keep the books, handle accounts payable and receivable, manage cash flow, etc.

Once I had found the dream team and the right people to fill these roles, I felt I could lay a strong foundation for the future. And this foundation would serve as the catalyst for growing the business exponentially over the next 10 years. This was the beginning of the future.

In addition to helping me create this foundation, hiring these key people also freed up more time for me to focus on the bigger picture, which is something you can't do if you're trying to play multiple different roles at a time. I'm more of a visionary, and if that's the case for you, then as you start to grow, you need to delegate. This can be difficult at first, but it is something that you need to get good at. Delegating allows you to have the vision, set the goals, know exactly where you want to get, and monitor your progression along the way via benchmarks.

And that's what happened. The departments I created continued to grow and we went from five employees to 35. I had the people that I could trust, which allowed me to focus on doing the work that I needed to do to build a foundation to grow.

How to Find a Good Team

You're likely wondering how you can find a team that is full of the right people that you can trust. And this begins with a lengthy interview process.

In my case, we worked with recruitment agencies that helped us screen folks for the various positions. So, by the time they made their way to an interview with us, they had already been screened so we weren't starting from scratch. This is a massive time saver.

With a list of potential candidates, we started a three or four interview process, with different people interviewing. Once everyone got a chance to interview the candidates, we convened together to see how everyone felt about the interview and how they evaluated the qualifications. I brought in some of the managing partners and one of the attorneys to participate in the interview process so that we had a well-rounded panel.

During interviews like this, it's important to ask questions relevant to the candidate's experience and see what they know, but it's also important to look for someone with a good personality. This is especially true for positions that are client/customer-facing, such as the person for our intake department that was on the phone most of the day with distressed people – people who had been in an accident, harmed, and didn't know what to do. It's key to hire someone that can handle phone calls that are often difficult so the person that made the call can feel like they're getting the help they need.

You also want to look for candidates who have been at various businesses for years, not someone who has been bouncing from place to place every six months or so. Even if they make sound good and look good, chances are good that they will also stay at your business for just six months or so. Ideally, you want someone who has been with companies for at least three to five years. This shows loyalty.

The interview process also involves taking various tests that test not only the person's IQ but what their knowledge is in regards to the position. If they pass these tests, then you hire them and move on to the next phase.

The Six-Month Plan

In this phase, you put them on a six-month plan of where you want them to be, set some goals for them, and be diligent about monitoring their progress along the way. For example, with the paralegals at the law firm I was working at, each has about 20-30 cases they're working on at a time and they have to be able to develop those cases and move them along within a certain amount of time. Developing the cases looked like getting the cases done on a timely basis as well as their mannerisms over the phone. So much of this job (and others) is about interactions with the client regularly, maybe even daily at the beginning and those interactions need to be professional, sympathetic, and helpful. I monitored their progress essentially by looking at their productivity.

To help them get to this point, we would conduct a lot of training meetings with role-playing, so to speak, that taught them what to say and to understand the verbiage used. We would listen in on the calls to see how they were handling the "client," whether they were asking the right questions and whether they were coming across as someone who cared and was knowledgeable. That was done for a period of time and then weekly meetings were held to go over the individual calls and let them know what they did well, what they need to work on, and more.

This is along the lines of what we did for other departments as well, as any role we were hiring for in the firm had some level of client interaction.

This six-month trial period was a good indicator of where things may go in the future. If things were not going well, it was time to let them go and find someone new. And if things seemed good, then it was time to reevaluate their position, their pay, and more. For the law firm, we would see if they were in a position for a raise or other incentives down the road. Raises are crucial for employee retention. You should pay your best employees a premium so they'll want to stay. In addition to potential raises, we would also potentially re-negotiate their healthcare coverage and look to additional rewards.

It's one thing to hire good people, and it's another thing to keep them on board. Simply paying them a salary is not enough.

With something like law, you can't give these employees a piece of the company, but you can give them incentives to make sure they know they are wanted and needed and are part of the family. So they are partners, in theory, so to speak, and are recognized for their work.

One of the ways to incentivize people is by giving them a bonus. With the intake department at the law firm, if an individual employee signed up, say, five new clients in a week, they would earn a certain bonus. If they sign up 10 new clients, they get a larger bonus. It's amazing how much of an incentive cash bonuses can be to people.

How to Know When It's Time To Scale Up Your Workforce

It's important to incentivize your current employees but you also want to be diligent about ensuring they aren't overworked. You can do this by evaluating where things are at and determining whether you need to do more hiring and scale up your workforce.

If you are getting more calls, it may be time to hire more people. As we hired more people at the law firm, we were able to move cases a lot more quickly, which meant more revenue. And that extra revenue we were able to put into marketing, primarily via television and radio at that time. By continuing to get the word out there in the masses via multimedia, we grew the business and along the way, expanded those departments.

We focused on checking monthly to see if we were meeting our quota and whether we had the right flow of cash coming in. This would help us determine whether we had the right number of people doing the right number of jobs.

Mistakes Are Part of the Process

However, the lessons above did not come without mistakes. But I don't know if any business owner, business manager, or entrepreneur has ever gotten to their position without making mistakes along the way. It's all trial and error and you learn from your mistakes.

It's common to try to grow *too* quickly and have to pair back. That's something we experienced at the firm. Too much money was going out and not enough money was coming in. That often leads to layoffs (which was the case for us), or at least putting employees on furlough. And that's part of the growing process and pains as well.

It's natural for businesses to expand and contract, so you always have to get together as a team and figure out what the next step is. Often those next steps require adapting to the new environment and the world around you. In the case of the law firm, 15 - 20 years ago, everything was done on notepads, and today, there's software for each step of the process. That was a major shift in the business when things when digital. And those advances are only going to continue to happen, across all industries. So you have to technologically keep up with the times to maintain your growth, and always be open to learning.

Learning was what took me from being a CFO to focusing on marketing and advertising. I unexpectedly found something that was interesting to me and that I enjoyed doing, and eventually found a way to turn that passion into a business of my own.

So when you get the urge to try something new, follow that urge because you never know where it may lead you. Just don't try to take the whole journey all by yourself.

CHAPTER 16

HOW TO GET THE BOARD TO SEE YOUR FUNCTION AS STRATEGIC, NOT JUST TRANSACTIONAL

By **LARRY PHELAN**

As a function head in a large organization, it can be difficult to make executives sit up and take notice of what your function is doing.

Within a business that has numerous functions, we're all pulling in the same direction to help the business move forward. However, we're also competing internally, trying to make our functions indispensable.

Along with the team and EY Consulting and Strategy and Transactions client servers, I have been able to make this happen for the Supply Chain Services (SCS) function at EY. This did not happen overnight.

However, in the eyes of the board-level executives, we were able to transition from being a function that felt at times like its only role was to buy enough printers to a trustworthy function that understands the direction the organization is growing and that fuels the growth.

Now we are an invaluable part of the EY organization. The board-level executives don't just rely on us to replace printers anymore.

Ultimately, any function in the business can follow many of the same processes we used to become the go to function when they need something done right.

There are five areas of focus that worked for our SCS function that can help you gain notice for your function at your organization.

Socialize, Socialize...And Then Socialize Some More

Convincing those at the board level about the importance of your function, takes constant communication.

You need to raise awareness of the job you're doing. At a board level, executives may not have a clear understanding of what your function does.

When I started working in SCS at EY in 2009, formerly known as Procurement, the role of the function was far different than it is today. I like to say that "procurement" started with a lowercase "p" at EY, because that's how our executives saw it.

You would go out and "buy printers" when you needed them. "Buy paper" when you needed it. Make selections and decisions in a vacuum without considering the overall effect on the organization. Just try to save money wherever you can.

At the ground level, the business was more than happy to keep procurement in the corner and to have it operate in the same way it had for years.

Our job was to take our "procurement" function to "Procurement," to raise awareness of what we could do, and transform it into a robust SCS function.

In the beginning, we needed to be able to show why working in a different manner than procurement had done for 30-plus years was going to deliver better results.

We needed to show the business the value of making these changes. We needed to show how these changes we were proposing would lead to improvements in the future. To do this, we used data analytics, the science of analyzing raw data in order to make conclusions about that information, to back up the changes we were proposing.

Then we held conversation after conversation, driving home the points we were making and showing how valuable our function could be as this new, transformed service.

This may sound difficult, and it can be. However, it will work, and our SCS function at EY is proof.

Be Prepared to Be Relentless

Gaining the approval for changes like we were proposing was not an easy process. Some executives naturally tend to resist change.

Our entire team had to be relentless to make the changes in SCS happen at EY. I'm not talking about being relentless in a manner that antagonizes executives, however.

Being relentless in this case involves using data analytics to discover trends that can help the business. And then bringing discussions to the board level about the changes our function could deliver, backing up claims with data.

Bringing innovative ideas with enthusiasm was important, however they were delivered with rock-solid data behind them too.

As you are in the process of making these proposals, be prepared to receive criticism and dismissals of some of your ideas. You need to avoid having thin skin. Don't take dismissals personally.

Being relentless isn't always an easy process. Some at the board level will resist you. However, keep bringing data and facts to the discussion and keep showing how your work is improving the overall performance level of the business.

My philosophy regarding being relentless is that I know everyone at the board level will not be receptive to this process. They may not really care about what we do.

However, I also know that even if executives have no interest in SCS, as long as we are keeping them informed about what we do and how we're being successful, they will respect what we are doing.

If only those executives who appreciate our function pay attention to us, this doesn't solve the problem. Even those who may not like my relentless attitude or who may resist change still need to understand what we do and how we are helping the organization.

Having a relentless attitude worked so well at EY over the past decade-plus that I now sit on a global service group that consists of 125 of the top leaders at EY.

This provides me the opportunity to speak with other executives who are working within the various services and functions, giving me additional ideas to integrate into our plans to support the business. Which in turn, gives our SCS function more credibility within the EY organizaion.

Drive Mindset Change in the Business

One of the toughest aspects of delivering change in the business involves changing people's mindset.

To migrate SCS from where we were at EY in 2009 to where we are today, took a strategic shift for the organization. It was important to convince executives at the board level about the importance of this with data and facts.

As a starting point, we wanted to show that changing SCS couldn't only be about trying to save money. Driving change in SCS also needed to involve things like solidifying the supply chain.

Should one supplier experience problems with geopolitical issues, developing an SCS strategy within the business allows for having other options for suppliers ready to go.

To achieve success in this area, we had to dig into the data from the beginning. In 2009, we needed to figure out what we spent with certain suppliers. We needed to understand the length of the various contracts we had in place.

This data was available, but we weren't collecting it in a way that made it easy to digest. We needed to organize the information to use it in a meaningful way.

By bringing multiple dimensions to the data, we developed the ability to begin making accurate predictions about the direction of the organization's growth.

One of our greatest achievements is the breadth that the SCS team helped deliver to the entire EY organization. We created a true supply chain strategy that strengthens the entire business.

For example, we took on real estate management for EY. The organization has around 800 offices spread across the world. Management of these properties costs quite a bit annually.

We quickly understood the importance of using our data in helping the business find the right pieces of real estate at the right price. We use our real estate properties to promote our brand, which is an efficient use case.

Some executives would say that if our team was willing to take on real estate, we should take on the facilities management piece too. After all, they are closely related.

However, we understood where the business stood at that time through our study of data analytics, and we knew the business was just not ready for us to take on that function.

A couple of years later, the business continued to reinvent itself and show progress, and this migration meant we were now ready to deal with facilities management. This is part of the ongoing process of reinventing ourselves.

Those are just a few examples of how we drove change over the years.

The work we did previously is paying off handsomely now. When other functions need to make a decision, their first thought is to check with the SCS team to access the data analytics we have in place.

Because we help deliver successful answers for so many segments of the business, other functions trust us. They begin to rely on us even more, and it becomes a continuing cycle.

We take advantage of this to show those at the board level how valuable we are and how we are constantly striving to improve. We put out reports regularly that showcase our data, showing the direction in which the EY organization is moving.

In fact, we don't always wait for other functions to come to us to seek the information any longer. We bring relevant data directly to them, giving them insights that they didn't even know they needed.

Finally, we constantly reinvent how we do things from a SCS level. Even when things seem to be running as smoothly as possible,

I always emphasize searching for ways to improve the process or expand what we're doing.

We never want executives at the board level to feel like we've fixed the SCS process and they can go back to ignoring it. We want to have improvements that we can share with the executives on a regular basis. We want to bring a new story to them as often as we can.

Focus On Exceptional Support

If your function isn't directly making money for the organization, it needs to be invaluable in its support of the functions that DO make money, which in the case of the EY organization is our client servers.

In SCS, this means focusing on how we can improve speed to market. We need to give functions across the EY organization what they need as quickly as possible so they can serve the clients without delay. For example, if we cannot obtain a piece of software we need to properly serve EY clients, we may lose out on the opportunity to retain the clients' business.

Our SCS team needs to look at the current position of the business and to anticipate where the next growth areas will be. We need to figure out whether we have the infrastructure available to accommodate these growth paths. That's the job, and that's what makes us valuable.

If we do not anticipate EY teams' need to have certain pieces of software available to serve EY clients, and it takes us a couple of months to obtain the software, the business falls two months behind.

We must prevent this lag from occurring.

Within SCS, we make use of multiple data points. We collect data as we complete projects. Using this data allows us to measure speed to market.

Did we help deliver the needed software and other equipment in time to make a difference? If not, how can we improve? If we did deliver on time, what tweaks can we make to deliver even better results the next time?

We can create brand value through these exercises and by constantly striving for improvement. Things like improving speed to market and mitigating risk through the techniques we use in SCS help deliver the brand value we're seeking.

To translate this to any aspect of the business, start by using data analytics as your building blocks. Studying this information not only gives you a snapshot of where the business stands at this point, it also helps you begin to predict the next steps the business should take. Do not be afraid to leverage experts, as referenced earlier, EY Consulting and Strategy and Transactions were my sounding board.

As you make predictions based on the data, track which predictions are the most accurate. These are the threads to follow as you make additional predictions.

SCS at EY has changed significantly from my early days. However, some organizations' SCS functions continue to operate in the same way we did a decade-plus ago.

What I often find when speaking with executives in a similar position to mine at other organizations is that they understand the general ideas behind our process. However, they want to fast forward to where our SCS team is now at EY.

It's important to remember that reaching the end state successfully doesn't just happen. It requires following certain steps. You can't just snap your fingers and make it happen. It takes a willingness to work hard at developing the best methods and processes.

Those at the board level then need to see the process work. They need to see you build up credibility over time to buy into the process. Building confidence in the process will yield the end results you're seeking.

Our techniques translate outside of SCS to other functions within the EY organization and can help your function become the one on which everyone else relies.

Make sure other functions know what you do and make sure they trust your techniques, making your function indispensable. If you can do that, the board will see your strategic value –no matter how transactional your function may seem on the surface.

EY | Building a better working world

EY exists to build a better working world, helping to create long-term value for clients, people and society and build trust in the capital markets.

Enabled by data and technology, diverse EY teams in over 150 countries provide trust through assurance and help clients grow, transform and operate.

Working across as surance, consulting, law, strategy, tax and transactions, EY teams ask better questions to find new answers for the complex issues facing our world today.

EY refers to the global organization, and may refer to one or more, of the member firms of Ernst & Young Global Limited, each of which is a separate legal entity. Ernst & Young Global Limited, a UK company limited by guarantee, does not provide services to clients. Information about how EY collects and uses personal data and a description of the rights individuals have under data protection legislation are available via ey.com/privacy. EY member firms do not practice law where prohibited by local laws. For more information about our organization, please visit ey.com.

© 2021 EYGM Limited.
All Rights Reserved.
EYG no. 000728 22Gbl
ED None

The views reflected in the introduction and this chapter are the views of the author and do not necessarily reflect the views of the global EY organization or its member firms.

ey.com

CHAPTER 17

ALWAYS SAY YES

By **LENORE GREGSON**

Always say yes, even if you're not sure at first when or how you're going to get there or how you are going to do it. Every door to every business or personal opportunity begins with that acceptance of the challenge. This chapter will explore why and how to say yes to everything, with examples from my health management and fitness coaching careers. I'll also offer advice on what to do if you feel like you've dug yourself too deep by committing to something, a situation we all find ourselves in from time to time. The bottom line is that when you commit to saying yes, you're committing to your success.

1. Why you should always say yes

If someone is asking you a question about your business, it's because they're in need of something. It's great if it's a product or service that you already offer – then saying yes is easy. But so many times, potential customers will ask us to do things that seem outside of the ordinary or outside of our comfort zone. Why should you say yes? Because if one person needs something, there are probably countless others who need it too. The bigger companies may not be able to offer it, and by saying yes you fill a void in the market that they can't. Suddenly you'll have not just one new customer, but plenty who have the same need but just haven't articulated it.

I'll give you an example from Kaiser Medical Management. During the pandemic, many companies weren't allowing their employees back to work unless they had a negative COVID test. One of these companies asked KMM if we could do at-home COVID testing for their employees. We'd never done that before, or even considered it, but of course the answer we gave was yes. So now, we offer a 10-minute and 15-minute rapid COVID test that is administered by a nurse at the employee's home. We even offer it on-site at the employee's workplace as well.

We could have easily turned the companies down, saying it wasn't in our purview or something we had any experience with. But then we would have allowed that customer to go onto the next health provider until one said yes to them, and we would have lost the opportunity. We have to be the ones to say yes.

In fact, the main reason Kaiser Medical Management has grown is because of saying yes so many times over the years. Every time a company asks me to do something for them, the only reason I haven't done it yet is that I haven't thought of it. For example, we used to have a doctor who did vitamin shot clinics while he was at our health fairs. When he stopped doing the fairs, people kept asking, "Where's the doctor who has the vitamin shots?" And so we started offering vitamin shots ourselves. Now it's one of the most popular services we offer to companies we work with.

Success is all about filling the voids when you notice someone else stopped doing something or notice no one's done it in the first place.

Sometimes, the reason to say yes is as much to help yourself as to help a customer or someone else. As part of my job at KMM, I run a fitness website and blog. It connects my work in health management with my other passion of professional weightlifting and bodybuilding. When people say yes to fitness, they think it'll change them on the outside. But really, it changes them more from within – "inside out," I like to say.

Towards the end of my fitness programs, I ask participants to share their stories of the time they've come to a fork in the road, one that would lead them in totally different directions in life. I've heard harrowing stories about abortions, rape, drug addiction, and incarceration. One woman spent three years in federal prison in a 6 X 6 cell with 6 other female inmates.

When she told me she was having a tough time with the fitness program and didn't know if she'd be able to complete it, I reminded her of all that she'd already overcome. Was she really going to let pushups and situps break her after spending three years living in a six-by-six room? That was the motivation she needed to keep going, and her reason for saying yes to herself.

2. How to always say yes

In many ways, saying yes is the easy part. But what comes next? It can be terrifying to commit to something you and your business have never done before, with the expectation of a promise on your shoulders. To get rid of that fear, you need to put a plan in action.

Right after saying yes, the first thing I do is put pen to paper. I ask myself what I need to do exactly to meet my goal, and then I just chip away at it until I've checked everything off the list and it's accomplished. There's no dillydallying – I just set my goals and conquer them.

I've had to say yes to two enormous projects during my time at KMM. The first was for a grocery store chain who wanted us to set up a health fair at every single one of their stores. This would normally be pretty manageable, except they wanted us to hold the fairs all on the same day and all at the same time. We had to provide all the tables, and for a small company like mine it simply wasn't cost-effective. When all was said and done, I ended the contract with the grocery store. But it was only because I said yes at first that I learned a valuable lesson and discovered my limitations and where I needed to grow.

Saying yes to a daunting school Covid testing project, on the other hand, was a huge success. A Texas school district wanted Covid testing for all their locations throughout Texas at the same time, so we had to hire contract employees and train them. It took about 45 days to prepare for the big Covid testing day, but when it finally rolled around it went off without a hitch. I never would have imagined completing such a project until I was asked about it and said yes.

A few years ago, someone on the fitness blog said that they'd like a program to be able to go through the same thing I do before a bodybuilding show. Of course I said yes, and that's how I came to start the nine-week fit challenge. It's inspired by the work I put into my gym routine and my diet in the nine weeks before a stage day. My company offers it to entire companies and their employees, but also just to regular folks.

The idea is for average people to get off the couch and see if they can make it through my routine for those nine weeks. I can't guarantee to someone that they'll look like a professional bodybuilder after they've completed it, but they will certainly be a better version of themselves. The program has changed so many lives — it's gotten people off of cholesterol medications, staved away pre-diabetes, and even helped someone shave off 70 pounds in one instance.

But it's not always easy for people to say yes to the fit challenge. One woman I spoke to about it went on about her friend in the program — how amazing she looked, how much weight she'd lost — but there was one sticking point. "I don't think I could eat like that," she told me. That's a case of someone who's already setting themselves up for failure, someone who just isn't ready yet.

Nothing happens in a comfortable state of being. If that was the case, we would all be couch potatoes and eat whatever we wanted and still be in incredible shape. No, it takes a certain amount of sacrifice, discipline, and time spent outside of your comfort zone.

Often when we say yes, it's saying yes to discomfort. When you're ready to stop feeling comfortable, change will happen.

3. I've said yes — now what?

Now, I'm not saying that everything is easy after you've said yes or committed to something. In fact, the follow-through is often the hardest part. It's so common for people to get to the middle of their task, after they'd said yes, and get down on themselves. Maybe they've tried their best and nothing is working yet, or maybe they think they shouldn't have said yes in the first place.

This is a regular occurrence in my nine-week fit challenge. It's only nine weeks, but many participants have never been through such a disciplined lifestyle in terms of diet and exercise. About half-way through, they're ready to throw in the towel and call it quits.

But when I touch base with them, their gripe usually isn't with the program as a whole – they generally enjoy working out and eating healthy, and especially the progress that comes with it. They often take issue with one small part of the challenge and get hung up on it. For example, one of the participants told me she thought about quitting because she just couldn't stand egg whites.

In those situations, where a pet peeve is going to make or break your commitment, it's ok to make small modifications for the good of the greater goal. I told her she could substitute egg whites for cottage cheese in the morning and get just as much protein. After that permission, she finished the rest of the fit challenge without complaint. Sometimes all it takes is a little flexibility to make sure you're able to continue saying yes to the big things.

No one can always say yes without support. I've been a professional bodybuilder for 17 years. Many people assume that with so much experience, and as a coach myself, that I don't have anyone to guide me along. In fact, I've had a dedicated coach I've worked with for all 17 of those years. Why? Everyone needs someone to hold them accountable when they say yes.

Think about professional athletes. Players like Tom Brady and LeBron James have been playing in the NFL and NBA for most of their lives, getting paid hundreds of millions of dollars along the way, yet they still have a myriad of coaches, trainers, and support staff. Even the brightest stars need someone to call them out on their commitments, so we all certainly do.

Another reason some people might be hesitant to say yes, or to continue saying yes, is a fear of failure. It's only natural, but I think it's irrational. Failure is like the boogeyman in the room – people are afraid of something that hasn't happened yet or may not ever happen. Does anyone ever pay attention to who lost the Super Bowl? That team failed at something, but down the road barely anyone remembers it.

There's nothing in my life that I regret, because the few things I haven't succeeded in have taught me something. Going in, I know every experience, every trial, every yes, is either going to be a success or a lesson. So when you fail, just move on and learn from it, because just like a lost Super Bowl, no one's going to remember.

What people will remember is your success, and you'll surely have a lot of it from always saying yes.

CHAPTER 18

YOU ARE WHAT YOU DO, NOT WHAT YOU SAY YOU WILL DO

By **PREETI TANWAR**

I distinctly remember the feeling - the excitement, the adrenaline rush, the self-satisfaction that came with overachieving. I was working at a startup, wearing multiple hats, sometimes as a Project Director, many times stepping into the shoes of a QA Tester, or stepping out of the office as an Account Manager to pacify unsatisfied clients. Some days, I was the collections person and on other days, I was an influential business development executive, working to raise over $1.25M as seed investment just by leveraging my inner social circle.

I really did it ALL and that too with passion and a smile, as I believed in the vision of this company. I also had my eyes set on the future that was promised to me - a lucrative salary and a board member position. And yet sadly, unlike the male members of the team, I didn't receive these things. I did not get what I deserved. Moreover, I was also not offered any justification or explanation for this decision.

I felt betrayed, having sacrificed time with my family and other career opportunities to join this startup. But I did learn a valuable lesson that day: "You are what you do, not what you say you will do!" From that point on, I knew that if I ever ran a business I would follow the policy of always following through and keeping my word.

Why don't people do what they say they will do?

I've noticed that the majority of the time, overcommitment is the most common reason for people to not show up or deliver what they have promised. We presume that we have to be perfect and say yes to every opportunity and every person. In reality, honesty garners more respect and leads to better outcomes for everyone involved. We all need to be proactive and let each other know when things aren't on track. As long as you have the right intention, communication is the key to setting clear expectations and building trust in a relationship.

I am not saying I am perfect! I make mistakes and don't always do what I say I will. But I have become much more aware and intentional to earn the trust of my team and my clients.

I've also seen how my own business and my team can be impacted if I don't do what I say I will. Lately, we've been having daily Scrum calls to discuss our latest project. The purpose is for everyone to briefly share the progress and the blockers. It provides a space for accountability and motivation, along with the collaborative spirit that comes when we're all working on smaller parts of a larger goal. When I fall back on my commitment and miss some meetings, I can sense a decline in employee morale. A team member might be ready to show me a new feature, but if I'm not there to see it, what is their motivation for making the next feature? These small actions add up over time to have a big impact.

Doing what you say you will isn't always easy. The key is to commit to doing things that align with who you are as a person and what you want out of life. To do that, you must find your purpose, define your values and priorities, and adopt the servant leadership model.

Find your purpose

Imagine you're going on a vacation. You've packed your bags, made it to the airport, and saved up enough money to take yourself to any destination in the world. The travel agent asks you where you'd like to fly to. "Just give me any flight," you say. "I've got so much money in my pocket and my summer and winter clothes packed — you can send me anywhere!" Do you think she can give you the right ticket? She will sell you a ticket, but the chances are pretty low that you'll end up in the best spot for you.

Now, imagine the same scenario, but this time you tell the travel agent you want to go to Hawaii or an island like it. You're going to end up much happier when you choose the right destination for yourself!

Life is just like planning a vacation: Being prepared helps, but knowing where you are headed is essential. Many highly competent people set themselves up for failure by not being clear about where they want to go. To know where you're headed, you've got to find a purpose for it and align your goals respectively.

I've been lucky to know from early on that my calling was to impact lives by mentoring students—my whole professional life has been geared toward guiding and coaching others. Since high school, I have tutored or counseled other students from my neighborhood because I felt good when I saw them do well. I enjoyed counseling them one-on-one to help them overcome their academic fears, which in turn helped me overcome my own personal inhibitions and made me a more confident person.

When I came to the US, I became the go-to person for aspiring international students or US women immigrants, trying to figure out their career goals. When I saw them struggling to find the right job or programs or colleges, that initiated the spark that eventually led to creating the Career Munzill platform today. I did all of the above along with working a full time job and taking care of my family. Helping others achieve their career goals brought me inner joy, peace, and fulfillment that fueled me to pursue my purpose.

It can be difficult to have a clear sense of purpose in many careers, but we all must keep looking, either in our day job, at home or by committing to a hobby or volunteer work. I think you have to take the time to introspect and ask yourself: Would you do it even if someone didn't pay you? Would you do it if you were sick or had to work odd hours? For me, the answer is a resounding "Yes!" to all!

My entire company is geared toward this same purpose of impacting lives by guiding people to grow in their careers. We help recent college graduates across the globe—especially women, immigrants, and first-generation students—and provide them with the information technology work experience they need to get a good job.

Along with helping me live out my purpose, my company, HiEd Success, helps staff and others find their own purposes. Every summer, I run a 12-week Ambassador program for college students to find their ideal role in the information technology world. Our students leverage a behavioral assessment platform where they can enter their preferences and receive a recommendation on which paths to pursue based on their skills and interests. Once they have an idea of their career targets, they get a better picture of which colleges to attend and which degrees to pursue. When the metaphorical travel agents of life come asking where they'd like to go with their futures, they have clear answers to go along with their qualifications.

If you're still looking for your life purpose, remember that it's not going to pop up out of nowhere. I started out doing only coding, but I knew there was something missing. It was only when I came out of my shell that I rediscovered my purpose of mentorship. I like to remind myself and others: There's no growth in the comfort zone, and no comfort in the growth zone. You have to go out and connect with people and try different experiences until something just feels right. You can't get that feeling by reading books or listening to other people. It's about action—and the more you do it, the closer you get to defining your life's purpose.

Know your Values and Priorities

Years ago, I was a "yes" person to a fault. I said yes to every-thing—my family in the United States, my family in India, my friends, and of course my business. I got myself into trouble with conflicting commitments before I finally realized that I couldn't make everyone happy all the time. I had to say no sometimes but to whom and to what? For that, I had to figure out a clear set of priorities.

Before you can set up a hierarchy of your priorities, you have to know what's valuable in the long run in your life. This knowledge makes it easier to make tough decisions in the short term. But, it takes quite a bit of reflection, and often some trial and error. I'm someone who hasn't always had the easiest time balancing my personal and professional lives. As an ambitious entrepreneur, I've personally seen the challenges that can arise at home, when we become so focused on our careers. These difficulties unfortunately multiply if you're a woman entrepreneur and grow exponentially for moms. Almost on a daily basis, I had to make the decision of what was more critical on that day and learn to live with the constant mommy guilt of not always being there for my kids.

I've learned that instead of pitting my personal and professional lives against one another, I need to recognize their interaction. As a workaholic, I toiled constantly at my company when it was first starting up, leaving little room for family time. Even though I was with my family physically, mentally and emotionally I was tied to unfinished work rather than being present in the moment.

That's how I realized that in order to truly prioritize my family, to really be there for them with my whole mind and heart, I needed to take care of my business first. I've struck a balance by prioritizing work unless it impacts my children. If competing priorities come, I have always included my kids with work rather than picking one over the other.

During school holidays, I had to pitch some important clients during a lunch meeting but needed to watch my kids as well. I ensured my son and daughter were sitting parallel to us at lunchtime while I finished my presentation. In fact, the client enjoyed meeting them and included them in our conversation. My kids were so motivated and started appreciating the efforts that I was putting into my new youth empowerment project, Career Munzill. All the anxiety of that morning trying to juggle responsibilities turned into a great bonding experience with my children.

I've found that decisions about my professional life are easier for me, as there are more facts and fewer emotions in business than dealing with friends and family. At work, the simple question I ask myself is, will this help my company grow or help me understand my team members better? If so, I take the opportunity without hesitation as long as the opportunities also align with my company's mission. I then create checklists and schedules of the business commitments at the top of my priorities.

Be the Servant Leader

To me, my goal as a leader is to serve! I believe in putting the needs of the employees first so they can develop and perform at their best. I provide opportunities for my team to grow and they are well aware that I consider not only clients but their own personal success as my success. They feel comfortable sharing their intent to work for a larger company given their earned experience at HiEd which I don't consider a loss. I'm proud that my guidance has had a positive impact on their careers. This has helped me to create long-lasting relationships with team members and clients alike. I have created long lasting relationships.

Effective guidance isn't always just about correction. Sometimes, people just need to be reminded that what they're doing is the right thing! I often send personalized notes to each of my team members to let them know what they're doing well. I let them share their personal stories in a group setting to reconnect at a deeper level with the team so even if the differences occur over time professionally, no one could hold grudges towards each other personally.

Last but not least, stand up for your employees. Recently, some tension occurred due to racial discrimination with a client. Standing up for what's fair, bringing it to the client's attention respectfully, and demanding equal respect both ways ensured the team members that their work and their existence both are respected.

As you go about your week, I challenge you to pay close attention to how you feel. Do a gut-check. A clear sense of purpose helps us wake up in the morning ready to take on another day. Priorities that line up with your purpose will enable you to function better and be more productive. And, if we've put in the time to establish values that are truly important to us, they will serve as guide rails during difficult situations. It is this alignment and awareness that will help you live out the philosophy that you are what you do, not what you say you will do.

CHAPTER 19

MORE THAN SECURITY GUARDS: HOW VETERANS MAKE GREAT EMPLOYEES IN ANY INDUSTRY

By **SCOTT SHEARIN**

Veteran hiring has been a popular and widespread topic for many years. Even with a recent shift to a broader focus on diversity and inclusion overall, many companies today are happy to onboard military vets into their ranks.

The Problem

I've worked in recruiting for 17 years, and I always hear what an abysmal job the Department of Defense (DOD) does at transitioning military vets to civilian life. Is that statement accurate? Yes. It is accurate. The DOD does in fact do a very poor job at preparing military folks appropriately for civilian life. The resources they do provide offer very little value to either the Vets transitioning or the folks looking to hire them on the other side.

My standard response? Thank goodness for that!

Seriously. If the military were regimentally effective at transitioning vets to civilian life, then just about all of us veterans would be security guards or police. True, the basic skill sets of security and police work are the foundation of what most vets learn, and a lot of us do successfully enter those fields. But there's so much more to the veteran talent pool.

Civilian hiring practices have the same problem, only in reverse. Those responsible for hiring decisions on the civilian side often lack confidence in facilitating hiring due to their personal perception of the military and what these folks were doing during their time there. In other words, many civilian HR managers disqualify veteran candidates for positions not directly related to a "military" skill set because they believe ex-military are only qualified to be cops and security guards.

In my thirteen years in the military, I worked in cryptography and intelligence. Would I, as every automated skill translator on the market tells me, make an outstanding security guard?

Well, I probably would...but I have no interest in that kind of career. I dreamed of being a stockbroker, failed out of college, got into the Marines due to being really good at taking tests, studied cryptography as an enlisted Marine and was commissioned as an intelligence officer, finally became a licensed stockbroker after leaving the military, parlayed that into selling life insurance, discovered I was way too cheerful to enjoy telling people they're going to die all day every day, then got into recruiting through an old Marine friend who was looking for a veteran who had sales experience. Where in all that would you get "security guard" or "cop"?

An individual veteran's journey cannot be determined with a collectivized, top-down solution, either on the part of the military bureaucracy or of civilian skill set evaluations. If we're being honest, nobody's journey can. Not one single element of the diversity and inclusion world can be solved through top-down models and one-size-fits-all programs.

So what's the solution?

The Solution

You might think I'm about to suggest mandating companies to hire more veterans. After all, I own and operate a recruiting firm specializing in veteran recruiting. Trust me, I would benefit greatly if a government forcefully mandated that all companies hire a certain percentage of vets into their workforce.

But no, this is not the way. Not only because force is immoral, but rather because that solution wouldn't derive the anticipated or targeted outcome regardless. That mandate would essentially make things far worse for the entire community.

And while I certainly don't speak for vets, I can say with confidence that the many that I know well would never want to be hired simply because someone thought they legally had to offer them a job.

Here's the real solution: understand that hiring veterans isn't something you need to be forced to do, it's actually something you want to do. You want us on your team. You just may not know it yet.

Case in point: when interviewing a veteran, it's great to pursue a deeper understanding and ask probing questions and even deliver technical assessments to gain confidence in that candidate's level of knowledge before further pursuing them for a position. You want to make sure this vet will be a good fit for your company.

Here's the kicker though. You already do that with non-veteran candidates as well.

So the idea that their experience doesn't translate to civilian work, an idea that acts as a roadblock to making more veteran hires, simply isn't true. That would be like choosing any random company outside of your specific industry, stating accurately that you don't fully understand how that company/industry functions, and then assuming that no one from that company could ever be a good employee in your industry.

There might be positions you have available that require specific industry experience, and that's fine. For those roles, a transitioning vet might not fit...but neither would anyone else outside your specific industry. So the problem is not that they're a vet. The reality is that a veteran's military experience likely means very little in relation to what type of candidate you have applying for your role and their ability to become an outstanding employee for your firm.

Most veterans didn't choose their job in the military. Their MOS (Military Occupational Specialty) was assigned to them when they enlisted. Just because a veteran was assigned an MOS as, let's say, a diesel mechanic, doesn't necessarily mean they enjoyed working as a diesel mechanic. It also doesn't even indicate that they were even any good at it. It's just the job that they were ordered and assigned to do.

The reality is, veterans are just as diverse as non-veterans. There's no shortcut to understanding them as candidates for your company.

Interview them. Talk to them. They will tell you all about their military experience and what they enjoyed, what they didn't, the things they excel at, and the things they don't. Their journey in the military was more of a learning experience than anything and what they did learn could be invaluable to your team!

Leadership

One of the core elements that make veterans so attractive to civilian firms is leadership experience. Leadership is a tough skill to come by when making hires.

What defines a leader in your organization? If one presented themselves in an interview, would you recognize and act upon it? How do you develop soft skills and build leaders internally?

Are you willing to invest the operational time to teach the technical if the candidate has those soft skills? If you are willing, do you have a defined plan for training?

The great thing about veterans is that they already understand leadership--at the least, how to follow and respond to it, and often how to be leaders themselves.

Shortly after a 4-year stint in college and in the middle of an 8-year marriage to the Marine Corps, I accepted my first position in corporate America as a broker in training.

It was during one of our infamous early Monday morning staff meetings that I was called upon by one of my favorite people, one of my first civilian supervisors who went by the nickname Hammer.

"Speaking of management Scott, tell us how the Marine Corps trains managers."

Stuck with no preparation and confronted with a room full of seasoned brokers and a small handful of newcomers like me, I was shocked when my answer came so immediately.

After a brief pause, perhaps more for effect than anything else, I replied:

"The Marine Corps doesn't train managers, Hammer, we train leaders and know good leaders will figure out how to manage on their own."

If you want a visual image of what Marine Corps Leadership training might look like in your world, it would go something like this:

- You call your entire team, one at a time, at 2 a.m. on a Sunday morning, let each one know there has been an emergency that requires immediate attention, and to meet in the conference room at the office in 60 minutes. Then hang up the phone offering no further explanation.

- 60 minutes later, sit in the conference room and see who shows up. Next, provide simple instructions for a group task that will need to be accomplished on a tight deadline. Make something up. For example, there is an immediate and unannounced audit. The annual budget needs to be developed and submitted for review by noon tomorrow so leadership can be prepared to present Monday morning. You have nine hours to get this done. We're all counting on you.

- Leave the room before questions can be asked. Go into the mechanical room, cut off the electricity, and turn on the fire alarm. Sit back and observe.

Amidst the chaos that ensues, someone, or perhaps multiple people, will stand above the rest and direct action. The finished product that is created by noon that next day might be horrific, it might not even come close to the product you requested. Doesn't matter. What you learn from this exercise and what is demonstrated in the actions of your team is invaluable.

If you do this repetitively, which the Marine Corps does, eventually you will begin seeing leadership traits develop in the most unlikely places. Team members will learn from previous experience. Watch others get things done and build their own confidence.

Let's be clear. In today's litigious society, I DO NOT recommend actually facilitating this training exercise. You can, however, create safe and rewarding exercises that borrow from the ways in which the Marine Corps identifies and cultivates a culture of leadership.

Ultimately, what you'll find is the real trick in creating leaders is not trying to figure out how to develop; instead, look for ways to allow leaders to discover and reveal themselves.

This is the perspective and experience of leadership that veterans will bring to your company.

PTSD

Another common concern for many with hiring Vets is the stigma associated with PTSD.

First things first. Let's strip that "D" from the equation right from the start. Post-Traumatic Stress is just that, "stress." It is the NATURAL reaction of a HEALTHY brain to unusual or uncommon stress. It is not, in any way, a disorder. The vast majority of those dealing with PTS are not people with combat experience, simply because combat is only one of dozens of different traumatic experiences people can have. You would never approach a person who had been mugged or just experienced a horrible car crash and claim they have a disorder.

PTS is not in any way a veteran-specific issue. PTS is said to affect roughly 7.7 million Americans, and we have 1.6 million post-9/11 veterans in existence. Even if every single member of the military, post 9/11, dealt with some aspect of PTS they would only account for 20.7% of all PTS sufferers--and the true number of veterans suffering from PTS is between 5% and 20% depending on which studies you follow.

For the sake of argument, let's say that 15% of veterans have PTS. That would equate to 240,000 post-9/11 veterans, or 3.1% of all Americans who have PTS. And given that there are roughly 156,000,000 people in the aggregate American labor force, any given hiring manager has only a 5% chance of hiring someone, anyone, regardless of veteran status that suffers from PTS. Your chances of hiring a veteran with PTS? 0.15%.

Veterans suffer from PTS at nominally comparable rates as non-veterans. When considering bringing veterans into your organization, PTS is not and should not be a required part of the equation.

Plus, there are many resources in existence making recommendations on how to accommodate employees who suffer from PTS,

vets and non-vets alike, and dealing with these issues is less prob-
lematic than you might believe. Mostly it involves being empathetic
and trying to understand what that employee is experiencing and
allowing that individual time to seek treatment.

Veterans Rock

Bottom line, veterans make great hires, create positive ROI, and
generally are important influences on company culture.

Funny thing, the exact same sentence can be written about any
classified grouping of people who are seen as outside the norm, be
it by ethnic background, gender, or sexual preference.

Not many debate the tangible and measurable value of developing a diverse workforce. You can see strong evidence of this in
many studies. This is the reason the diversity and inclusion industry
has risen to prominence over the past decade or so.

And while it's popular to latch on to the notion of justice or pun-
ishing those who do wrong through one's subjective lens, the reality
is that those companies who do not make the effort, voluntarily, to
strive toward diversifying their workforce punish themselves. Should
they continue operating in ways directly detrimental to the health of
their business (such as avoiding diversity) they will, over time, lose the
capacity to compete within their respective industries.

In other words, don't hire veterans because you think you should
or because you're afraid of getting into legal trouble if you don't. Hire
veterans because veterans make great employees--and not just in
the security sector.

CHAPTER 20

REBUILDING TRUST IN HEALTH CARE THROUGH STRATEGIC COMMUNICATIONS

By **STEPHANIE LIMB**

A weird thing happened during the COVID-19 pandemic. On one hand, hospital and nursing home physicians, nurses, and staff were feted as heroes. Signs popped up in parking lots proclaiming, "heroes work here." Parades of cars flashing their lights and honking their horns drove around hospitals to celebrate the selfless, hard-working staff inside. Companies from Krispy Kreme and Adidas to Lyft and Verizon offered free or discounted meals and products to nurses and other frontline workers.

At the same time, vitriolic, sometimes violent, opposition to the medical and public health communities' guidance on how to manage the pandemic and slow the spread of the virus swept across the United States and the world. Masks, vaccines, lockdowns, even the existence of the virus itself were subjects of disagreement. And the opposite of the hospital car parades took place, with people shooting highly selective videos of their local hospitals to present an image that they were doing just fine and not overrun with patients. According to The Conversation, the conspiracy-based #FilmYourHospital social media trend generated 22,785 tweets by 11,333 users in a single week.

So while there was very visible and demonstrative support for frontline workers, a large proportion of the population believed the virus was a hoax and that hospitals and their teams purposefully perpetuated lies in order to make money.

We would be naïve to think these tactics were propagated by the fringes of our society and were therefore harmless. In just 15 months, between March 2020 and June 2021, Facebook removed more than 20 million posts from both Facebook and Instagram, which it also owns, for violating rules on COVID-19 misinformation. What these data do not reveal is how long these posts were up, how many times they were viewed, or how many times they were shared before they were removed.

The social media giant also added information labels to more than 190 million other COVID-19-related posts informing users that third-party fact-checkers had rated the information posted as false or missing key context. Again, who knows how many people viewed and/or shared the information without the warning label before it was flagged? It's certain that irreparable damage to credibility was done before the offending posts were removed or identified as misleading.

The changing guidance from the very institutions we ordinarily trust on issues related to public health, including the Centers for Disease Control and Prevention, Food and Drug Administration, and Department of Health and Human Services, made convincing people of facts about the situation even more challenging. The federal government's changing, and sometimes conflicting, guidance around social distancing and masking, for example, created the perception that no one really knows the science and that whim--or worse, political agendas--were driving the nation's public health policy and approach to curbing the virus's spread. And while these changes were understandable given the novelty of the coronavirus and the struggle to respond to it in real time, they tended to confuse people more than convincing them.

The Ostrich Approach

Amid this chaotic environment, some health care leaders decided the whole situation was too politically charged and that the best approach was "no comment." A prime example of this approach is the county public health director for Walla Walla County in Washington state. When asked by a local restaurant owner if he should require masks for his staff and customers considering the changing recommendations from the federal and state government, the public health director didn't take a position.

In an interview with NPR's All Things Considered in August 2021, the public health director explained his ambivalence by saying, "I'm not a PR man. I don't have a degree in communications.....People have their belief systems, and sometimes I sit around, like, what was one thing I would say that would change their mind? And I'm not convinced that I have the ability and power to do that." He elaborated that his reticence to communicate on divisive topics, such as masks and vaccines, is rooted in his desire for people not to "hate" public health once the pandemic ends and instead feel able to trust it.

Following this logic, communicating on difficult health care topics could only further undermine the public's trust in public health institutions and leaders. The only way not to alienate the public is not to take a position or offer professional judgment, no matter how well-informed or based on data and evidence that position might be.

The Too Little, Too Late Approach

A second approach to pandemic communication was taken by the well-intended North Texas physician who leads the North Texas Mass Critical Care Guidelines Task Force. In an effort to proactively deal with dwindling hospital bed capacity during the summer of 2021 COVID-19 surge fueled by the Delta variant and the unvaccinated, the task force prepared a memo outlining how clinicians could ethically deploy "crisis standards of care," as well as if and how COVID-19 vaccination status could be considered fairly in the allocation of care resources.

A phrase rarely heard outside of the academic bioethics community, "crisis standards of care" refers to legal and ethical guidelines for health care providers to decide who gets care when not everyone can get care due to resource deficiencies and shortages. It's an alternative way of describing the rationing of health care resources.

The leak of the memo almost immediately generated pushback and raised questions about fairness and perpetuating racial and economic injustices. The task force's leader and document's chief author quickly backpedaled, calling the memo a "homework assignment." This statement implied that the document was a theoretical exercise rather than the articulation of ethical and clinical guidelines to equip physicians with actual tools to make fair decisions under impossibly difficult and emotionally challenging circumstances. And then he reversed course altogether, saying that vaccination status shouldn't be considered when rationing care. Tellingly, he also told the *Dallas Morning News,* "We're trying to decide how to explain this addition [of COVID-19 vaccination status to the crisis standards of care] to the public."

After the flurry of opposition and the task force's equivocation, the memo died on the vine, and there was no subsequent conversation about fair and equitable care rationing, despite the number of available ICU beds plummeting to almost zero for the entire Dallas-Fort Worth region.

Missed Opportunities

The unknown author of the aphorism, "a lie can travel halfway around the world before the truth puts on its shoes" (or its pants, depending on to whom one attributes the saying) would be heralded a prophet in today's era of disinformation. But prophecy isn't written in stone. The truth can prevail. The solution is not to let the lie get a head start and to make sure the truth puts on its shoes faster.

While the examples above might be the results of well-intentioned behavior, they both represent regrettable reluctance to lead on the part of health care leaders and the triumph of misinformation as a result. Each represents gigantic missed opportunities for desperately needed leadership through better communications strategy and tactics.

In the public health director's case, while formal training in PR or communications may have been lacking, that cannot be an excuse for not engaging with the public and offering an assessment or recommendation based on the science, particularly when there is confusion and questioning. Without his direct engagement on masks and vaccines, his community was left to navigate very swampy waters on their own, possibly at great and unnecessary risk to their health. Worse, his not engaging in a tactful manner handed the microphone to those with flawed knowledge, exaggerated claims, and ideas rooted in conspiracy. The result was and is an emboldened stream of already dubious information and an ever-growing cycle of confirmation bias.

In the Dallas physician's case, he had a great opportunity when he was challenged on the crisis standards of care memo to reach the public with clarity and confidence. He could have explained why and how the memo came about, what crisis standards of care are (and are not), and how he and his department were actively considering fair allocation of care. Without this explanation, we were left only with narratives that hospitals are leaving patients to "rot and die," as alleged in an April 30, 2020, Facebook video.

And, in both cases, their communications and engagement needed to be immediate, frequent and repetitious. The fact that they weren't hurt both their leadership capabilities and the larger public view of the pandemic and how to respond to it.

We need more trusted voices, not fewer, speaking up on health care topics. Conversations on health care issues, whether masking, vaccines, Obamacare, Medicare for All, or any of a number of other policy topics, will occur no matter what. Health care leaders, in both the public and private sectors, who do not communicate to their staff, patients, and communities on these admittedly challenging issues cede the ground on these conversations to less-informed voices pushing their own agendas.

Rebuilding Trust Through Communications

As a nation, we will continue to process the lessons of the pandemic for generations to come. A thorough analysis of the government's response will be essential to avoid any further erosion of the public's trust and confidence. In its latest poll of Americans' opinions on the federal government, the Pew Charitable Trusts found just 42% of Americans thought the government does a somewhat good (31%) or very good (11%) job of effectively handling threats to public health. Overall, trust in the federal government has reached a historic low: just 20% of Americans say they trust the federal government to do what is right always or most of the time.

These numbers obviously reflect trends and factors that go way beyond missing or confusing messaging and communications, and getting the government into more favorable territory will take time. Nonetheless, health care leaders would be remiss not to double down on regular, consistent, and authentic communication as a major part of rebuilding the public's trust in science, government, and health care institutions and facilities and the people who are part of them. Part of that communication is also acknowledging missteps, course corrections, or changes to guidance that happened because new data or evidence were introduced.

Our country has a decent track record of post-crisis analysis. Commissioned study groups including the Warren Commission, the 9-11 Commission, and the Iraq Study Group, for example, while not without political undertones, still provided insightful facts for future leaders to consider and offer a roadmap for how we might address the current pandemic's tragedy of miscommunication and disinformation to avoid repeating it in the future.

From medicine to public policy, health care is complicated. Continuing to hide behind that complexity as a reason not to engage or explain, however, only adds to the opaqueness–and ultimately to public frustration and distrust.

How to Communicate Health Care Issues Effectively

As we've said, health care issues are complex. It simply isn't possible to explain in under 30 seconds why the U.S. has approximately 30 million residents without health insurance, for example. Likewise, explaining the science behind vaccine development and approval would take more time than most people have or are willing to spend to understand. Nonetheless, it is possible to influence knowledge, shift mindsets, and motivate a specific behavior or action with an effective communications strategy.

From our work with a wide variety of health care clients that includes hospitals, technology companies, and advocacy organizations, the keys to effective communications are:

1. **Know your audience and adjust your language and vocabulary accordingly.** "Interdisciplinary," for example, may mean a lot to physicians but absolutely nothing to a potential patient who assumes as a given that physicians across specialties communicate and work together.

2. **Eliminate all jargon or insider language.** A legislative audience, for example, has to track, monitor, and be conversant on countless policy issues, not just those related to health care. As complex as health care is, so are agriculture, oil and gas, and immigration. This audience will have a different comfort level with detailed technical language than an

agency regulatory analyst. Using language that is not imme-diately accessible alienates your audience.

3. **Break the issue down into discrete, consumable compo-nents.** Communicating on a policy issue or selling a digital health care tech product means more than rattling off a list of technical details or product features. Communicating clearly starts with establishing the core value propositions and artic-ulating the problem and solution the proposed policy or product offers. Next, communicate in discrete, consumable pieces. My business partner always says, "eat the elephant one bite at a time." Good advice. Establish a cadence and editorial calendar for how each message will be scheduled and delivered and following #7 below, re-delivered.

4. **Don't focus only on external audiences.** Share the infor-mation and key messages with internal staff so they can be champions in their own communities and families, and the knowledge spreads organically.

5. **Steer clear of conjecture, opinion, or personal spec-ulation.** Replace phrases like "I think," "I believe," or "in my opinion" with "the science tells us," "we know," or "the answer/solution is." And, if you don't know, don't guess.

6. **Be clear. Be consistent. Be precise.** The best advice I ever got on writing was to prioritize the editing process. Make sure that every word is purposeful, accurate, and in the ser-vice of your message. And then do it again.

7. **Repeat. Repeat. Repeat.** You may get tired of hearing

yourself repeat your core value propositions and key messages, but audiences are bombarded with information and need to hear messages frequently and consistently for them to stick. The research on marketing and communications suggests that a frequency of between 7 and 20 times is needed for message "stickiness," and the more complex the message and the more crowded the space, the more frequent the communications should be.

8. **Use all available communications channels.** While your audience may not be on Tik Tok, they likely are on YouTube, which is the world's second most used social media platform, with 2.29 billion users in 2021. Maybe YouTube feels odd for you to consider, but the key here is not to let personal bias inform which channels you use. Make your choices based on the data, not your personal preference or belief.

Health care complexity isn't going away. There's also no shortage of voices or channels to push messages on complex health care issues that are inaccurate, flawed, oversimplified, or incomplete. Countering heated rhetoric with authentic messaging is the responsibility of all trusted health care leaders. Post-pandemic, rebuilding confidence in the health care system will require a commitment to communications as a key executive and C-suite function.

CONCLUSION

By **ADAM TORRES**

Business leaders come from many backgrounds. Their stories are infinitely varied. Along the way, they experience success and failure. Some of the leaders presented are further along their leadership path than others, but one common trait is shared among all of them. They are never done working on their craft. They continue to push forward to test the boundaries of what they think they are capable of. Above all, this one trait will be responsible for much of the innovation that occurs in our generation and the generations that follow. Leadership is fundamental to our future success, not only in business but in our society at large.

To your success,

Adam Torres

P.S. If you'd like to apply to be a guest on one of our shows visit **MissionMatters.com/PodcastGuest** to apply.

APPENDIX

Adam Torres | Introduction | Page iii
Co-Founder Mission Matters
MissionMatters.com
Instagram: @AskAdamTorres
Twitter: @AskAdamTorres

Adam Nager | Chapter 1 | Page 1
Serial Entrepreneur
adam@medicalbillingopportunity.com
www.medicalbillingopportunity.com
www.adamnager.com
https://www.facebook.com/adam.nager.9

Alan Pawlowski | Chapter 2 | Page 11
President, Pace Management, Corporation
Partner, Next Point, LLC.
Partner, Health Strat Solutions
https://www.linkedin.com/feed/
https://www.pacemc.com
alan@pacemc.com
https://www.nextpointllc.com
https://www.healthstrat.com

Allan Hilsinger | Chapter 3 | Page 23
Founder and CEO, Guard Well Identity Theft Solutions
ahilsinger@guardwellid.com
www.guardwellid.com
www.guardwellcredit.com
https://www.facebook.com/allan.hilsinger
Allan Hilsinger (@GuardwellID) / Twitter
https://www.youtube.com/channel/UCaIU1UZ4qf0u0LKt0JkSb1A
https://www.linkedin.com/company/guard-well-identity-theft-solutions

Arnold Volker | Chapter 4 | Page 33
Founder of Inventor U
President and Owner of Next Innovations
Arnold.volker@inventor-u.com
https://www.facebook.com/InventorU
https://www.facebook.com/nextinnovations
https://www.inventor-u.com/
https://www.linkedin.com/in/arnold-volker-1865a715/

Charles Christopher Tyrrell, Esq. | Chapter 5 | Page 41
CEO of Tyrrell Law, PA
ctyrrell@tntvisa.com
(305) 433-7677
YouTube: TNTVISA
FaceBook: Tyrrell Law, PSC
Instagram: Tyrrell_law
LinkedIn: Tyrrell Law, PSC

Demetra Bakas | Chapter 6 | Page 49
Founder & Managing Director, Finance & Accounting Recruiter at Madison
Street Search
Website: www.madisonstreetsearch.com
Email: demetra@madisonstreetsearch.com
LinkedIn: www.linkedin.com/in/demetrabakas

Derek Gerber | Chapter 7 | Page 59
SVP, Explainify
derek@explainify.com
www.explainify.com
derek.gerber@calibearmedia.com
www.calibearmedia.com

Don G. King | Chapter 8 | Page 67
Chief Executive Officer, Impact Workforce Solutions
dking@impactws.com
www.impactws.com
https://www.linkedin.com/company/impactworkforcesolutions/mycompany/
verification/.

G. Cole, ARM, CLC | Chapter 9 | Page 75
Author, Founder, Creator of NeuroEmpowerment, Brainwave Analyst, Mental Health Consultant
info@empoweredg.com or g.cole@supermind.us
EmpoweredG.com
pathwaveslife.com
supermind.us
https://www.instagram.com/pathwaveslife/
https://www.facebook.com/pathwaveslife/
https://twitter.com/PathwavesLife
https://www.linkedin.com/in/g-cole-89678a10a/
https://www.youtube.com/channel/UCsazubiTRkTOUyIP9NYyNMg

Jason Shupp | Chapter 10 | Page 83
President and 3rd generation of Ferguson Roofing Co. Inc.
jshupp@fergusonroofing.com
LinkedIn: www.linkedin.com/jason-shupp

Jeff Norskog | Chapter 11 | Page 91
VP of Strategy & Development, Genyous Biomed
jeff@jnorskog.com
https://www.linkedin.com/in/jeff-norskog-032a882

Jeremy W. Hunt | Chapter 12 | Page 101
Founder & CEO, MN Delivery Solutions
jeremy@mndeliverysolutions.com
Facebook: @jeremywhunt, @mndeliverysolutions
Instagram: @jw.hunt, @mndeliverysolutions, @truthstream_
LinkedIn: jeremywhunt

Jessie Williams, MBA, CPA | Chapter 13 | Page 111
CEO & Managing Partner of jmWilliams CPA, LLP
JESSIE@JMWILLIAMSCPA.COM
LinkedIn: https://www.linkedin.com/in/jessiewilliams-cpa/
Facebook: https://www.facebook.com/williams.jessie
Facebook: https://www.facebook.com/jmwilliamscpa
Instagram: @jmWILLIAMS, CPA LLP
https://www.jmwilliamscpa.com/

Jim Downes | Chapter 14 | Page 119
Founder of Blueprint CFO & Fractional Chief Financial Officer
Website: blueprintcfo.com
Email: jim@blueprintcfo.com
LinkedIn: linkedin.com/company/blueprintcfo/
Instagram: @blueprintcfo
Facebook: @blueprintcfo
Twitter: @blueprintcfo

Joseph Catania | Chapter 15 | Page 129
CEO & Founder of Catania Media Consultants LLC
CFO of Catania & Catania, P.A.
jc@CataniaMedia.com
jcatania@CataniaandCatania.com
www.CataniaMedia.com
Facebook.com/cataniamedia/
Linkedin.com/company/64622339/admin/
Instagram.com/cataniamedia/
Twitter.com/joecatania12

Lawrence (Larry) Phelan | Chapter 16 | Page 137
Chief Supply Chain Services Officer, EY Global Services Limited
larry.phelan@eyg.ey.com
www.ey.com/en_gl/people/larry-phelan
https://www.linkedin.com/in/larry-phelan-7262b255/
www.ey.com
Twitter: @eynews; @carmine_disibiio
Facebook: https://www.facebook.com/EY/
Instagram: ey_global
LinkedIn: https://www.linkedin.com/company/ernstandyoung/mycompany/
SlideShare: https://www.slideshare.net/ernstandyoung
YouTube: https://www.youtube.com/user/ErnstandYoungGlobal

Lenore Gregson | Chapter 17 | Page 149
CEO of Kaiser Medical Management
www.kaisermedicalmanagement.com
www.lenoregregson.com
https://www.facebook.com/KMMSouthTx
https://www.instagram.com/lenore_ifbbpro/
lenore@kaisermedicalmanagement.com

Preeti Tanwar | Chapter 18 | Page 157
HiEd Success & CareerMunzill Founder
preeti.tanwar@hiedsuccess.com:
https://hiedsuccess.com
https://preetitanwar.com/initiatives
https://careermunzill.com
https://www.linkedin.com/in/preetitanwar/
https://www.linkedin.com/company/hiedsuccess/mycompany/?viewAsMember=true

Scott Shearin | Chapter 19 | Page 165
CEO of Veteran Talent Advisors
Founder and CEO of Klimb (in development)
scott@veterantalent.com
LinkedIn: @Scott Shearin
LinkedIn: @Veteran Talent

Stephanie Limb | Chapter 20 | Page 175
Co-Founder & Senior Partner, Groundswell Health
Ourgroundswell.com
stephanie@ourgroundswell.com
LinkedIn: stephanie-limb-0a754463/

Listen to our
PODCASTS

MISSION MATTERS
WE AMPLIFY STORIES

www.MissionMatters.com

OTHER AVAILABLE TITLES

In the fifth edition of *Money Matters (Business Leaders Edition Vol 5)*, Adam Torres features 18 top professionals who share their lessons on leadership. In these pages, through inspiring stories, you'll discover:

- The real cost of bad customer service!
- How to truly become a mission-driven organization!
- Seven ways women can thrive in a male-dominated world!
- Why relationships, education, achievement, and love are true values in leadership!
- How imperative it is to tell your story!
- Why it is essential to teach children how to manage online purchases!
- And much more!

Purchase at **MissionMatters.com**.

In this latest edition of *Mission Matters (Women in Business Edition Volume 1)*, Torres features 18 top female professionals who share their lessons on business and leadership. In these pages, through inspiring stories, you'll discover:

- Why empathy and EQ is crucial in leadership
- How failure paves the way to success
- How to find your purpose
- How to turn your passion into your life's purpose
- What it means to turn challenges into gifts
- What value-based care means for cancer patients
- And much more!

Purchase at **MissionMatters.com**.

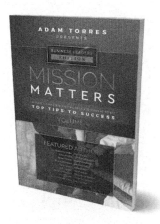

In the fourth edition of *Money Matters (Business Leaders Edition Vol 4)*, Adam Torres features 18 top professionals who share their lessons on leadership. In these pages, through inspiring stories, you'll discover:

- How patient care and technology meet in the medical field.
- How digital transformation is imperative for companies.
- What creating your dream retirement looks like.
- How to create a result-driven culture in your company.
- How to pivot your marketing to survive crisis situations.
- Why cohesion is more important than engagement in an organization.
- And much more!

Purchase at **MissionMatters.com**.

In the third edition of *Money Matters (Business Leaders Edition Vol 3)*, Adam Torres features 13 top professionals who share their lessons on leadership. In these pages, through inspiring stories, you'll discover:

- Different approaches to leadership and people management.
- Rules for success from a Green Beret.
- How to effectively manage a company full of millennial employees.
- How to transform your marketing mindset.
- Where customer success and employee success meet.
- What manifesting your success in business looks like.
- And much more.

Purchase at **MissionMatters.com**.

In the second edition of *Money Matters (Business Leaders Edition Vol 2)*, Adam Torres features 18 top professionals who share their lessons on leadership. In these pages, through inspiring stories, you'll discover:

- How to harness the entrepreneurial mindset.
- Why scaling your business for sustainable growth is vital.
- How to grow your eCommerce business.
- Lessons learned from sales experts.
- How to level up your leadership.
- How to manage your energy.
- And much more.

Purchase at **MissionMatters.com**.

Navigating the world of real estate can be stressful. Are you getting closer or further away from your goals?

Adam Torres is here to help you move forward. In his latest edition of *Money Matters (Real Estate Edition Volume 2)*, Torres features 13 top professionals who share their lessons in real estate.

In these pages, through inspiring stories, you'll discover:
- How to get more properties through syndication.
- How to implement servant leadership to have a more successful business.
- Why investing in real estate is not just for rich people.
- How important insurance is in real estate transactions and what to look for.
- Why using a private lender can help you in real estate transactions.
- What legal options you have to protect your assets.
- And much more!

Purchase at **MissionMatters.com**.

In the original edition of *Money Matters (Business Leaders Edition)*, Adam Torres features 15 top professionals who share their lessons on leadership. In these pages, through inspiring stories, you'll discover:

- How to create a clear path for growth.
- Why every business should act like a media company.
- How to build a community to last a lifetime.
- Lessons learned from professional soccer.
- How to maintain a well-connected brain for peak performance.
- How to create harmony through union in business.
- And much more.

Embracing diversity and inclusion in a rapidly changing business landscape can be challenging. Are you and your organization positioned properly for this new age of connectivity? Torres features fourteen top Asian leaders who share their lessons on diversity, equality and inclusion.

Navigating the world of real estate can be stressful. Are you getting closer or further from your goals? Finance guru Adam Torres is here to help you move forward. His guide, Money Matters, features 15 top professionals who share lessons from their more than 250 years of combined experience.

In this clear, concise manual, financial expert Adam Torres goes over the basics of personal finance and investing and shows you how to grow your wealth. Torres makes sure you are prepared for whatever life throws your way. It's never too early to think about the future and his book will give you the right tools to tackle it.

All books available for purchase at **MissionMatters.com**.

This workbook has been designed specifically for individuals like you who are dedicated to improving the results in all areas of your life. By following the ideas and exercises presented to you in this transformational workbook, you can move yourself into the realm of top achievers worldwide.

Download for free at **MissionMatters.com**